White Southerners

ETHNIC GROUPS IN COMPARATIVE
PERSPECTIVE • General Editor
PETER I. ROSE *Smith College*

Random House New York

White Southerners

Lewis M. Killian
University of Massachusetts

TO RICHARD W. ERWIN
Justice of the Supreme Court of Florida
A white southerner who in his career has exemplified the most gracious features of the southern gentleman as well as the vision and courage that offer the only hope for the emergence of a truly New South.

◉ Foreword

"Nation of nations" or "Herrenvolk democracy"? Melting pot or seething caldron? How does one describe the ethnic character of the United States?

The conventional wisdom, reflected in traditional texts on American history and society, tells of the odyssey of one group of newcomers after another who came to these shores: some of their own free will and others in the chains of bondage; some to escape religious persecution, others fleeing from political oppression, and many seeking their fortunes. "Rich and poor," goes the story, "mighty and meek, white and black, Jew and Gentile, Protestant and Catholic, Irishman and Italian and Pole . . . a motley array who, together, make up the Great American Nation."

Although many a school child can recite the litany, even they know that it has a rather hollow ring. For most people there are at least three kinds of Americans: whatever one happens to be, the members of the dominant group (viewed differently depending where one stands in the status hierarchy), and everybody else. And, if one happens to see himself as a member of the dominant group, the number of alternatives may be reduced to two: they and we.

For a variety of reasons writers of textbooks and teachers of American history have tended to overlook or underplay this essential fact of American life. While acknowledging the pluralistic character of the social structure and celebrating the extent to which "our differences make us strong," they rarely convey the true meaning of membership in an ethnic group. And none know this better than those whose life experiences belie the notion of tolerance for all. Recently, a common plea has arisen from various quarters: "Give us equal time."

In response to such demands there have been attempts to

alter the rather lop-sided image of American history and of the American people. Historians and social scientists have begun to respond to the call for a more accurate and meaningful view of race and ethnicity in America. Many have sought to "redress the balance," as they say, by upgrading the status of one group or another and rewriting their history to parallel that of the dominant group. One finds new volumes that appear to make the same strategic errors as those they wish to complement, i.e., placing emphasis on great events and prominent figures while avoiding in-depth descriptions of patterns of social organization, cultural traditions, and everyday activities.

Fortunately, there have been some other approaches tried recently, most notably studies seeking to reassess the entire ethnic experience not by playing the mirroring game (we have a hero, you have a hero; we have a holiday, you have a holiday; everybody has . . .) but by getting to the core of the social and economic and political realities of existence for the various peoples who came (or were brought) and stayed. The work of the latter scholars is far more important and, by its very nature, far more difficult. It involves new ways of looking, new perspectives. It encourages the examination of history and biography, of episode and event as before. But it also requires careful study of culture and community and character, the examination of everyday life.

Those who have and use such an imagination (C. Wright Mills called it "the sociological imagination") must possess a willingness to challenge the old homilies, to get away from stereotypes and deal with real people, and to relate that which is revealed with both detachment and compassion.

For a student to truly understand the nature of group life in the United States and the relevance of race, religion, and nationality as meaningful social categories (and critical social variables) he should receive two kinds of messages: those which help him to know, and others which help him to understand. This means that, if truly successful, writers of articles and books on the Irish in America, or the Jews, or the Black experience, should be able to evoke in their readers some sense of empathy, some visceral response to what it means to read a sign IRISH NEED NOT APPLY, or to hear the echo of "Sheeney,

Sheeney, Sheeney" ricochet off the walls between two old-law tenements, or to know what it is to be called "boy" by some and "brother" by others.

This volume is one of an original series written to provide student-readers with the sort of background material and sociological evaluation just mentioned. Like the others in this series, Ethnic Groups in Comparative Perspective, it offers information about the origins and experiences, the cultural patterns and social relationships of various groups of Americans. Taken together, the volumes in the series should provide a new and different look at the ethnic experience in the United States.

In planning the series it was decided that all books should follow a relatively common format which would include chapters on social history, descriptions of social organization of the various communities and their differing cultural characteristics, relations with others and with the wider society, and a conclusion to tie the early chapters together.

The very best qualified historians and social scientists would be invited to join in the venture, those not only informed but committed to the approach sketched earlier. Each author would be given the freedom to work within the framework in his own way and in his own literary style so that each volume would be a unique contribution to the overall project—and each could stand alone.

Daniel Aaron, a distinguished historian of and commentator on American literature, recently observed that the best writing of today comes from hyphenated Americans, members of such minorities as the Jews, the blacks, and white southerners. In the last instance, he was thinking of such novelists as William Faulkner, Flannery O'Connor, William Styron, and Eudora Welty. Their writings express the marginality of their subjects and their region. And well they might for, as Aaron suggests, white southerners, too, are a part of multi-ethnic America—a special part. This book is about them and their culture.

Lewis M. Killian, the author of *White Southerners* was born, raised, and educated in Georgia. Like so many of his kith and kin he served in the United States in World War II and remained a reservist, retiring in 1969 with the rank of colonel. Unlike many of his "cousins" he also broke with tradition, going up to Chicago to take a Ph.D. in sociology. His doctoral dissertation dealt with southern migrants and is still recognized as a landmark study. Killian is known for other work as well: *Collective Behavior* (coauthored with Ralph Turner), *The Racial Crisis in America* (written with Charles Grigg) and the penetrating and pessimistic volume, *The Impossible Revolution? Black Power and the American Dream*.

In his writing and teaching, in Oklahoma, California, Florida, Connecticut, and Massachusetts, Killian has maintained a love-hate relationship with his "homeland," while hewing close to the spirit of his mentors at Chicago, the first sociologists to attempt to "tell it like it is."

White Southerners is a portrait of a region and a people. In six short chapters, Killian sets the stage, describes the principal participants—white and black Protestants as well as the Catholics and the Jews, tells of those who stay behind and those who leave to seek new lives elsewhere. He then places his "ethnic group" in the wider context of American society.

Auslanders will learn much about the South from Professor Killian (like what people really thought—and think—of Jefferson Davis; why April 26th is considered "Memorial Day" in Dixie; how the myth of the southern gentleman emerged and became reified; how ambivalent the attitudes of blacks and whites toward one another can be and are . . . even what one does with "pot likker"). Northerners and southerners both will learn even more as they read this sociohistorical assessment of the Old Confederacy and the New South.

Lewis Killian once told me that, when he first came to the University of Massachusetts, he moved through a reception line for new faculty. Ahead of him were several Europeans. Despite thick accents, they were greeted without comment. When he got to the head of the line and introduced himself, he was asked if he longed for home. At that point, he reports, he did.

There are many strangers in the land—including white southerners.

PETER I. ROSE, *General Editor*

◉ Preface

The author is tempted to apologize for undertaking yet another interpretation of white southerners, for the literature on the South already seems limitless. In doing the research for this book I began to suspect that every white southerner possessed of any literary talent has felt impelled to interpret the South anew. As black writers have been preoccupied with the problems of their race, white southern writers have been intrigued by the mystique of their region. At the same time, many non-southern writers have been fascinated by white southerners and particularly by their faults.

In this abundant literature several "Souths" appear. One is the dark, mysterious land of prejudice, poverty, and decadence. This South has been treated as a wayward child of the nation by non-southerners and as a sick, but still beloved, child by white southerners, such as William Faulkner. To a school of writers who cherish the label "conservative," the South is neither sick nor evil. To them it is still the most American part of the United States. That which is distinctive and precious about the region in their eyes is its political conservatism, its aristocratic tradition, and its esteem for people and land rather than for technology. Writers of this school see the South as the last hope of America.

It is difficult to recognize this romantic, still-solid South in the writings of southern liberals, ranging from eloquent journalists and novelists to statistics-spouting sociologists and economists. They tend to see a progressive South, heterogeneous, changing, rapidly losing its regional distinctiveness and becoming more American. Every indication of change is seized joyfully as proof that the South is disappearing as a cultural region.

I have tried to avoid reproducing any of these stereotyped

portraits of the South and white southerners. It is impossible to write about so vast a region without doing violence to many of its complexities, inconsistencies, and nuances. Undeniably there are many Souths; yet the idea of *the South* persists. In examining white southerners as a group I have endeavored to keep in mind homogeneity and heterogeneity; continuity and change; group norms and individual attitudes. Above all, I have proceeded from the assumption that white southerners constitute a group, not just an aggregate of discrete individuals who happen to have been born in the same geographical portion of a nation of nations.

◉ Contents

Foreword   *vii*
Preface   *xi*
Chapter 1 • White Southerners   3
    The White Southerner Defined   10

Chapter 2 • The Southern Homeland   14
    The People   15
    The History of a Regional Psychology   17
    Southern Defensiveness   20
    The Legends of the Defeated South   21
    New Nation, New South   27
    The Industrialization of the South   29
    Stereotypes of the South   32
    The Negro in the New South   33
    The South Rises Again   37

Chapter 3 • Southerners: Rich, Poor, White, Black   45
    The New Middle Class and the Aristocratic
      Tradition   46
    The Decline of Agrarian Dominance   48
    The Effects of Urbanization   51
    Southern Conservatism, New Style   54
    Black Southerners   56
    Migration to Southern Cities   58
    Migration to the North   62
    Black Militance in the South   63
    The New Racial Order   64

Chapter 4 • Marginal White Southerners   69
    Catholics and the Civil War   70

Jews and the Confederacy   72
Jews, Catholics, and Southern Demagoguery   75
The Assimilation of Catholics and Jews
  in the South   78
Transplanted Yankees   83

Chapter 5 · White Southern Migrants   91
The Exodus of White Southerners   92
The South: An Intellectual Desert?   94
The Visibility of White Southerners   96
The Hillbilly Problem in the North   98
The White Southern Laborer as Hillbilly   102
A Case Study in Chicago   104
The Stereotype of the Hillbilly   107
Discrimination Against White Southerners   108
The Hillbilly Tavern   109
Reactions of White Southerners as a Minority   111
The Durability of the Hillbilly Minority   112
The Affluent Migrant   113
White Southern Pride   117

Chapter 6 · White Southerners in a Pluralistic America   120
Southern Fundamentalism   121
The Revival of Pluralism   122
The Quest for Minority Power   124
Local Self-Government   125
The Principle of the Concurrent Majority   126
Constitutional Guarantees   129
Secession   130
Two Ways for White Southerners   131
A Minority No More?   141
The Significance of a Quasi-Minority   142

Selected Bibliography   147
Appendix   153
Index   165

White Southerners

Chapter 1 ◉ White Southerners

This book is about white southerners, a sociological minority group in the over-all context of American society. Treatment of such a sizable group of native Americans as a minority may be challenged on logical grounds, to be sure. Since colonial times membership in this group has also constituted membership in the larger, English-speaking, white, Protestant ethnic group that has been dominant in the social, economic, and political affairs of the nation. The epithet "WASP"—white-Anglo-Saxon-Protestant—could easily appear to have been coined to describe specifically the white Southerner. Yet the term commonly refers to those white Americans of all regions who by accident of birth have been lucky enough to escape any of the stigmata that would place them in one of the conventionally defined minorities. A WASP may be a New England Yankee, a midwesterner of pioneer stock, or a native son of the Golden West. Nathan Glazer and Daniel P. Moynihan treat white, Anglo-Saxon Protestants in New York as a distinct ethnic group in *Beyond the Melting Pot*.[1]

The term WASP is not merely a label for a dominant but residual ethnic category in a nation of minorities. It also connotes unseemly ethnic pride and prejudice toward other groups. Because a common stereotype of the white southerner makes him the epitome of WASP bigotry, there may be an emotional opposition to treating him as a member of a minority. To ascribe to the traditional symbol of racial oppression any of the liabilities of minority status may seem somehow to make less distinctive and exquisite the suffering of "real" minorities. It will automatically suggest to many readers a defense of the white southerner when, in their minds, he has no defense and deserves no sympathy. But this very reaction, plus the fact that white southerners have, of all Americans, most unabashedly vaunted the whiteness of their skins and the antiquity of their Americanism, may suggest an important sense in which they do constitute a minority. As the essential WASP, the white southerner may be a special object of prejudice for non-southern members of the white, Anglo-Saxon, Protestant dominant group. Dewey Grantham, Jr., implies as much when he says, "The sectional theme may owe some of its vitality to the fact that many Americans have been able to externalize inner conflicts by focusing on the South as a deviant section."[2]

No amount of elaborate pleading will overcome the arguments that may be advanced *against* the proposition that white southerners are indeed a minority. At best, their status in the larger society is too anomalous to support clearly the contention that they are a minority and not merely a distinctive segment of the dominant group. That their actions, particularly in the political realm, have been one of the mainstays of white dominance in the nation as a whole is undeniable. Yet there is heuristic value in examining this segment of the dominant group as if it were indeed a minority group, perhaps best called a "quasi-minority." Certainly many of its members have acted at times as if they were members of such a group. Understanding the "minority psychology" of white southerners is essential to explaining their behavior as members of the dominant group in American society.

The late Louis Wirth advanced a definition of a minority that has since become classic. To him, a minority was: "A group of people who, because of their physical or cultural characteristics, are singled out from others in the society in which they live for differential and unequal treatment, and who therefore regard themselves as objects of collective discrimination."[3]

This definition points to two interacting aspects of minority status. One is the attitudes and actions of others in the larger society toward the members of the minority, the "differential and unequal treatment" that constitutes discrimination. Equally important, however, is the perception of the minority that it is the object of prejudice and discrimination. If such a perception led only to a feeling of being humiliated, down-trodden and powerless, intergroup relations would be far less acrimonious and violent than they are. Group pride not only dies hard, however; it often seems to be nourished in adversity. A group that is the object of discrimination or believes itself to be such may react by developing a defensive group consciousness that sets it apart even more and serves to preserve its distinctiveness. This defensiveness sometimes leads to an aggressiveness that seems almost paranoid—a quickness to take offense and a readiness to strike back at forces seemingly on the verge of overwhelming an already persecuted people. Hitler cultivated such a psychology in the German people, transmuting the defeat of 1918 into the seed of German aggression in World War II.

So it has been with the white South. For years many unsophisticated white southerners who had never seen a bluecoated Union soldier clung to the image of the Yankee as the ancient enemy who, no matter how affable he might be, boded no good for the South. Even as late as the 1920s many regional deficiencies were still charged to the account of the Yankee invaders, to defeat, and Reconstruction. In Georgia lone chimneys standing amid the ashes of burned-down shacks were called "Sherman's monuments." The image of the historic foe was constantly updated, however. Yankees were absentee mill-owners who paid low wages, charged high prices, and sent managers with strange, brusque accents to boss good southern laborers. They were tourists with big cars and bulging bankrolls who crowded the highways and left a trail of injured feelings during their annual pilgrimage to Florida. Some of them were a new version of the "Carpetbagger"—slick, unscrupulous hucksters who came South to bilk innocent southerners of their honestly earned wages.

Worst of all, Yankees were a vast, invisible mass of white Americans who, whether because they didn't understand Negroes or because of a perverted affinity for them, constantly threatened to destroy the basis of "good race relations"— segregation and white supremacy. They ate with black men and allowed their children to sit next to them in school. Although they were not kind to Negroes as southerners were, they encouraged them to develop false notions of equality by calling them "mister" and allowing them to vote. Furthermore, their representatives in Congress were constantly trying to complete the subjugation of the white southerner by introducing antilynching and antipoll-tax bills. Even the renewed sense of national unity created by World War II did not destroy the myth of an insidious campaign. During the war, countless white southerners believed firmly in the existence of "Eleanor Clubs" and "Bumping Days" (days on which every black was supposed to go downtown and bump a white off the sidewalk!).[4] Then the United States Supreme Court—"the Warren Court"—became the symbol of Yankee vindictiveness toward the white South. There followed the second invasion of the region, this time by a nonviolent but nonetheless reprehensible army of civil rights workers. Not only did the North send its agents to disrupt southern communities during their summer vacations; it infiltrated the student bodies and even the faculties of southern universities. It mattered little that many of the crusaders were themselves southerners "born and bred"; the presumption always was that "race trouble" was created by "outsiders." The latest version of the meddling, malign outsider is the Washington bureaucrat, typically from the Department of Health, Education and Welfare, who comes into a community for two or three days to tell the native authorities how they must manage their schools, hospitals, or welfare systems.

The belief of the average white southerner in these stereotypes has been encouraged and sustained by the rantings of southern politicians, from "Pitchfork Ben" Tillman to George Wallace. Such politicians have always included in their strategy exploitation of the support of a solid white South unified by fear of a perennial conspiracy plotted by the Yankee outgroup. The ancient battle cry, "states' rights!" has always carried a connotation of "regional rights" in the South. Whatever it might mean to politicians and voters in other sections of the nation, below the Potomac this slogan means "southern rights" and "freedom from Yankee interference." In his campaign for the Presidency in 1968, George Wallace proposed states' rights as a value to be cherished by all sections of the country. He made it explicit that people in other regions might do what they wanted with these rights. At the same time, he could be certain that his white southern audiences knew what he meant by states' rights for the South.

Unsophisticated southern citizens and shrewd, conservative politicians are not the only ones who have perceived white southerners as a minority constantly threatened with persecution. Some of the most liberal politicians and astute scholars the region has produced have subscribed to their own version of a conspiracy theory. Long before black Americans began to contend that they were a colonized people, the great, liberal, southern sociologist, Howard W. Odum, proclaimed that the South was still in the status of a "colonial economy."[5] Odum, it has been pointed out, probably only intended to denote the economic status of the region as one that furnished raw materials to other regions, which processed them and shipped them back as finished manufactured goods.[6] The theme that he enunciated came to be expressed, however, in a large body of economic and sociological literature arguing that the South was discriminated against in tariffs, railroad rates, and the allocation of capital investments. Some liberal politicians and journalists, such as Ellis Arnall, former governor of Georgia, and Jonathan Daniels, of North Carolina, brought this theory to the attention of a wider audience and revealed their own intuition that they indeed spoke for a minority that was "the object of differential and unequal treatment." Arnall, in *The Shore Dimly Seen,* not only described the South, along with the West, as the victim of a "colonial policy" designed "to maintain colonialism and a low standard of living."[7] He also described that South as "a minority," one of the minorities that Franklin D. Roosevelt had put together in the Democratic party. In so doing, Arnall classified white southerners as a "geographical minority," in a category with Catholics, the largest religious minority, and Negroes, the largest racial minority.[8]

As one reason for the "colonial" and "minority" status of the South, this southern white liberal voiced another theme with which his most reactionary opponents would heartily agree. "The aftermath of the War Between the States," he declared, "was the longest armed-occupancy of a defeated country in the annals of modern history."[9] Thus, despite their legitimate claim that the states of the Southeast were among the earliest members of the federal union, southern whites have long nursed a rankling sense of injustice and oppression because of Reconstruction. Despite the efforts of modern historians to debunk the southern version of the history of this period, the collective memory has been haunted by the images of boisterous black legislators, avaricious Carpetbaggers, misguided and unruly Negroes, and a noble Ku Klux Klan that should never be confused with its shabby imitators of later years.

Finally, Arnall revealed another facet of the sense of persecution shared by many white southerners, conservative and liberal. In fact, he suggested that southern white liberals suffered from this sort of discrimination more than did their reactionary compatriots. He asserted: " Liberalism in the South is handicapped by the attitude of a group of critics, who form a coterie of professional liberals, and who can find nothing in America to view with alarm except the atmosphere of the Southern states."[10]

Thus, even in the writings of one of the white South's greatest liberals are found overtones of the defensive group consciousness shared by white southerners of so many persuasions. Another southern white liberal, Ralph McGill, has explained this pervasiveness of the southern mystique:

> It is the fate of the Southerner to be involved in his region, always to feel himself held by it. He may never have believed the myths. The often cruel injustices of the rigid formula of race may have offended him and aroused him to open opposition . . . But nonetheless, he is a part of what he has met, and been. And the past, in tales of his grandparents, his great-aunts and uncles, has been in his ears from birth.[11]

But does "the mind of the South," with its legends, its pride, and its defensiveness, constitute anything more than a variant of the sectionalism found in any corner of the vast, heterogeneous union of sovereign states? In justifying the memorable title of his book on the subject, W. J. Cash contended that it did: "There exists among us . . . —both North and South—a profound conviction that the South is another land, sharply differentiated from the rest of the American nation, and exhibiting within itself a remarkable homogeneity."[12]

There are other sections and regions of the nation. There does not lie beyond the borders of the South one vast, undifferentiated region that constitutes the rest of the nation. The great regionalist Odum wrote first of the southern regions of the United States, but then he addressed himself to "American regionalism," examining the Middle States, the Northeast, the Far West, the Northwest, and the Southwest.[13] Frederick Jackson Turner argued that "in spite of similarity of traits and institutions throughout the nation, it is also a congeries of sections."[14] The people of other regions of the United States have a sense of a distinctive history and culture; they express pride in their natural resources, their cities, their industries, their political leaders. They conjure up their own regional grudges against the rest of the nation. At times "the East" seems alien and threatening to the people of the western regions just as "the North" is disquieting to southerners. Is the South truly so different?

The inescapable record of history and the persistence of certain cultural traits suggest that it is. Although some New England states once talked of secession, as southern historians will never let them forget, the South is the only region that ever withdrew from the federal union and claimed a separate nationhood. It is the only region that, for a long period of its history, was cursed with "the peculiar Institution" of slavery and that made enforced segregation by race a part of its legal system. There alone school children are taught American history from the viewpoint of a nation that lost "the War," a nation whose heroes were condemned as traitors and whose enemies were glorified in the rest of the country. Every state in the union has its state flag and official song, but the South is the only region in which people honor what was once a rebel flag and still rise for a second "national anthem." One must live in the South to appreciate the profound significance of "Dixie." When it is played, an individual may stand either to honor its symbolism or merely to go along with the crowd. If he fails to stand, however, he soon senses that he has committed an act of defiance. There was a time when, after the

North had made its peace with the white South and white supremacy seemed secure, standing up when "Dixie" was played seemed only a way of honoring the heroes of the lost cause of independence. When segregation began to fall before the onslaughts of the Supreme Court, however, honors rendered to "Dixie" and to the Confederate battle flag came to symbolize a different cause, one that many white southerners were not willing to regard as lost. Now to refuse to honor them signifies that one is not merely ignorant or unsentimental but that he is a traitor to "the southern way of life"—an integrationist. The minority psychology of white southerners has been revitalized.

The White Southerner Defined

Before we analyze white southerners as a minority, one question remains: Who is a white southerner? There is no easy answer, for it is even difficult to define "the South" as a region, and it has been suggested that, if white southerners are a minority, they are a regional minority. It would be presumptuous, however, for us to attempt to improve on Howard Odum's gargantuan effort to define the major regions of the United States on the basis of nearly 700 indices. Recognizing that there was no longer a single entity that could be called the South because of the emerging distinctiveness of the Southwest, Odum defined a southeastern region corresponding roughly to the Old South.[15] This region includes the states of Virginia, North Carolina, South Carolina, Kentucky, Tennessee, Georgia, Florida, Alabama, Mississippi, Louisiana, and Arkansas. When the South as a region must be discussed, it is these eleven states that will be encompassed by the term. (See Appendix, Chart 1.)

But what of the people? Not all white people who are born in these states spend their whole lives there, and not all who live there are born in the region. The "rule of descent" that Charles Wagley and Marvin Harris have suggested as one of the defining characteristics of a minority cannot be applied.[16] Instead, "white southernness" must be defined in terms of exposure to southern culture and of self-definition, a white southerner being (1) a white person who has been born and raised at least until young adulthood in the South and who still thinks of himself as a southerner, or (2) a white person who, no matter where he was born and raised, lives in the South and identifies himself as a southerner.

This is admittedly a loose definition. It excludes many white people from Texas and Oklahoma, particularly the eastern parts of those states, who may consider themselves as thoroughly southern as any native of Georgia or Mississippi. It also excludes many migrants from Missouri, West Virginia, and the southern portions of Illinois, Indiana, and Ohio who, in northern cities, find themselves classified as hillbillies and begin to think of themselves as compatriots of migrants from further south. These groups are excluded despite the emphasis the definition places upon the consciousness of being a southerner as an essential element of membership in the minority. If this emphasis was not an important part of the definition, however, an untold number of migrants to the South who have cast their lot with the region and come to love it and cherish its customs would have to be left out. To exclude them would be as unrealistic as refusing to call Sam Houston a Texan because he was not born in his adopted state. Finally, the definition deliberately excludes many white people who are born in the South but, who, after settling in another region, lose their identification with the South. Perhaps their number is not very great, however. It is not easy for them to forsake their southern heritage, nor do other people make it easy for them to forget it.

One reason for this is that the native white southerner is likely to carry with him for a long time a cultural mark of identity of a type borne by many national minorities—the southern accent. This is not essential to the labeling process when he goes abroad; in a nation of mobile people, every new-comer expects to be asked, "Where are you from?" The white southerner, however, expects to be asked at one time or another, "Where y'all from?" While the linguists may be able to identify other regional accents, and while specific localities within and outside the South have their distinctive dialects, no

American accent is so persistently associated with a regional culture as is the southern "drawl."

The definition of white southerner proposed above dictates that the members of this minority must be considered both at home, in their native region, or away from it, in other parts of the United States. A brief social history of the southern region will show how the South became different from other regions and developed a regional ethnocentrism that has become the basis of a minority psychology. Then, in analyzing the social organization and cultural patterns of the region, the diversity of population segments within the region will be considered. Not only are there various classes of white southerners, but there are also southerners who have other highly salient group memberships. This includes not only black southerners, but Jews and Catholics. It includes, too, those marginal white southerners who live within the region but whose "alien" origin has not yet been forgotten. Then also, in some parts of the South, there are the tourists, the seasonal invaders who arouse remarkably incongruous reactions from the natives.

Allusion has been made to the intuition of many white southerners that they and their region are the objects of prejudice and discrimination. The case for this belief will be examined. Here the diversity of the white southern population again becomes relevant. The problems, real or imagined, of the politician and the businessman are different from those of the white southern intellectual. As is true of the poorer members of many minorities, working-class white southerners provide the acid test of prejudice against the group. Thus special attention will be paid to the concept of "the hillbilly," a term that has a meaningful place in the vocabulary of many non-southern whites.

Finally, the place of white southerners in a nation that seems to be moving in the direction of a new mode of pluralism must be considered. For years assorted observers from both within and outside the South have predicted that someday the South—meaning the white South—would "join the rest of the nation." It has been a fond hope of some students of race relations that amelioration of the plight of the black southerner would come as the pattern of black-white relations in the South "caught up" with the pattern of other regions. In the light of recent developments in race relations, what the fulfillment of these predictions and hopes might mean is no longer so simple as it once appeared.

Notes

1 Nathan Glazer and Daniel P. Moynihan, *Beyond the Melting Pot* (Cambridge, Mass.: The M.I.T. Press, 1963), pp. 8–9.

2 Dewey W. Grantham, Jr. (ed.), *The South and the Sectional Image* (New York: Harper & Row, 1967), p. 2.

3 Louis Wirth, "The Problem of Minority Groups," in Ralph Linton (ed.), *The Science of Man in the World Crisis* (New York: Columbia University Press, 1945), p. 347.

4 See Howard W. Odum, *Race and Rumors of Race* (Chapel Hill: The University of North Carolina Press, 1943), Chap. IX.

5 Howard W. Odum, *Southern Regions of the United States* (Chapel Hill: The University of North Carolina Press, 1936), p. 219.

6 Clarence H. Danhof, "The Colonial South," in Grantham, *op. cit.*, p. 128.

7 Ellis G. Arnall, *The Shore Dimly Seen* (Philadelphia: Lippincott, 1946), p. 143.

8 *Ibid.*, p. 298.

9 *Ibid.*, p. 97.

10 *Ibid.*, p. 87.

11 Ralph McGill, *The South and the Southerner* (Boston: Little, Brown, 1964), p. 218

12 W. J. Cash, *The Mind of the South* (New York: Knopf, 1941), p. vii.

13 Howard W. Odum and Harry E. Moore, *American Regionalism* (New York: Holt, 1938).

14 Frederick J. Turner, *The Significance of Sections in American History* (New York: Holt, 1932), p. 183.

15 Odum, *Southern Regions, op. cit.*, pp. 7–11.

16 Charles Wagley and Marvin Harris, *Minorities in the New World* (New York: Columbia University Press, 1958), p. 71.

Chapter 2 ◉ The Southern Homeland

Although it is neither a political entity nor an isolated land mass, the South is a geographic region. An incurable romanticist or an adamant geographical determinist could wax eloquent about the effects of climate and topography on southern culture and the temperament of white southerners. To do so, however, would be to ignore the vastness and diversity of the region. The fertile flatlands of the tidewater, the humid swamps of the bayou country, and the hills and hollows of the southern Appalachians only begin to illustrate the range of climate and geographical environments in which southerners have lived.

The one variable inextricably related to the ecology of the area is the cotton culture, which, during the early part of the nineteenth century, spread from the eastern seaboard to the most western reaches of the region, distorting the economic development of the South and spreading slavery. Even those subregions into which cotton and slavery did not penetrate were touched by the blight, economically, politically, and socially. The people lived in the Kingdom of Cotton, where the planter class was at the apex of the social structure and the blacks were at the bottom, even below the slaveless mountain folk and poor whites. Except in Kentucky, white southerners who had never planted cotton, owned a slave, or favored secession were swept into the Confederacy when the states in which their voices were a minority left the Union to form a separate nation. After the abolition of slavery and the decline of the cotton culture, white southerners of all varieties found themselves fellow victims of war, defeat, and regional impoverishment. Most significantly, the long shadow of slavery left them inhabitants of a region that, for at least another century, had the lowest percentage of native whites in its population of any part of the nation even though the highest percentage of its white population was native born. (See Appendix, Table 1.) Cotton, slavery, secession, and "the Negro problem" comprise a complex of variables that has touched the life of every white southerner and that must be ascribed in part to the geography of the southern homeland.

The People

Just as there is variety in the geography of the South, there is a historical diversity in its white population. This diversity has been hidden by the assimilation of people of many national stocks in a relatively homogeneous caste of white southerners that stands in contrast to the other large bloc of southerners, the blacks. Yet the South was first settled by white immigrants with marked cultural differences, not just by Englishmen. The Scots and the Irish came from the British Isles, but there were also the French and the Spanish, whose influence can still be seen in New Orleans, Mobile, and parts of Florida. Germans and Swiss and French Huguenots sought religious freedom in the southern colonies, as did a small group of Spanish Jews invited by James Oglethorpe to settle in Georgia. But the coastal cities of the South never became great ports of entry for successive waves of immigrants as did New York and Boston and, later, San Francisco. By 1790 the South included in its white population a slightly higher proportion of people of English stock than did the rest of the nation, 62.7 percent as against 60.1 percent for the nation.[1] When white southerners of Scots or Scotch–Irish (Ulster Scots) descent are included, the Anglo-Saxon character of the southern white population in 1790 is even more evident. In the South, 81.3 percent of the white population was of English, Scots, or Scotch–Irish stock, as compared to 74.1 percent in the nation.

Cultural variations based on differences in national origin

began to disappear until the diversity of the original settlers was reflected only in place names. As immigration to the United States continued in the first half of the nineteenth century, the southern white population continued to become more and more "Old American." The competition from slave labor, the monopoly of the best land by plantation owners, and the absence of growing industries discouraged new immigrants from drifting south from the northern ports to seek their fortunes. Most important, the South did not experience the impact of new immigration after the Civil War in the way that the rest of the nation did. While the population of the Northeast, particularly, was growing by immigration, that of the South grew primarily by natural increase. Indeed, the region became an exporter of people to other parts of the nation, losing in every decade a greater number of white people by migration than it gained. (See Appendix, Table 2.) By this time the flow of immigrants from abroad to the United States had long since been restricted by federal immigration laws.

Thus, over many decades, the white southern population became stabilized as a relatively homogeneous Old American population, of predominantly English or Scots descent, with such diversity as it once possessed hidden by the remoteness of colonial history. Howard Odum observed in 1936 that the Southeast, "exclusive of its Negroes," was the most "American" of all regions.[2] The South was never to become part of the "melting pot" that, in the early decades of the twentieth century, gave the cities of other regions so much color and so many problems. (See Appendix, Table 3, for percentage of native whites in South.) Where there were hyphenated Americans in the South, the pressures for Anglo-conformity were greater than they were in any other part of the nation. The immigrant community was not a part of the southern scene. The great division in the South was between black and white. Southern cities had their Smoky Hollows but no Little Italies or Chinatowns. Spanish Ybor City, in Tampa, was an exception. The French Quarter in New Orleans was French only in an historic and commercial sense, not in terms of its living culture. For a southerner, the salient fact was and is whether he was white or black; all else was secondary.

The History of a Regional Psychology

Not only in terms of the composition of its white population but also on the grounds of its history the South can lay claim to being the most American of regions. Let it not be forgotten, says the proud and loyal southerner, that Jamestown was settled thirteen years before the Pilgrims set foot on Plymouth Rock, and that the oldest city in the United States is St. Augustine, Florida, settled by white Europeans in 1565. While most of the fighting in the Revolution took place in the North, it was at Yorktown that the British finally surrendered. Washington, the Father of His Country, was a white southerner and so were Jefferson and Jackson. Furthermore, the antebellum South was peopled not only by distinguished statesmen but also by brave soldiers, dashing cavaliers, and gracious ladies—the most romantic American types except for the frontiersmen, and the South also contributed its share of these.

Even during colonial days the idea of a southern aristocracy began to develop. In *The Mind of the South* W. J. Cash effectively branded this tradition as a myth.[3] He described the process through which the impoverished sons of the English gentry as well as some indentured servants built great plantations, constructed stately mansions, imitated the life-style of English gentlemen and transmuted their plebeian origins into a cavalier heritage. In the southern part of the land of freedom and equality the concept of an elite developed early.

Abetting and paralleling this development was the evolution of slavery and the American concept of the Negro. The question, "Who is a Negro?" is answered somewhat differently in every society that includes a black segment. As Negro slavery developed in the southern colonies, so also did the American answer to this question. Since there was no provision in English law for slavery, Africans were first held in bondage as indentured servants, a status they shared with some white Englishmen. Gradually, under the common law, the colonial courts defined a separate and distinct status for the slave. By the beginning of the eighteenth century, white indentured servants were declining in importance as a source of cheap labor while the use of African slaves was growing. Several factors contributed to this shift.[4] The white bond servant was an Englishman and usually a Christian, at least nominally. The African lacked even lower-class English culture and was a heathen; therefore he was not likely to receive even the modicum of consideration that the white colonist felt he owed a fellow Englishman and a fellow Christian. The black slave was not an English citizen and so "had no advocate and no protection as a citizen under English law" as did even the most abject white redemptioner.[5] Most important, the black servant had a visibility that the white servant lacked. If he became a runaway, no brand was needed to make him stand out in a crowd of free colonists. Since most black men were bond servants, the burden of proof that he was a free man rested upon the Negro; the "normal" status of the African in America was that of a slave.

This definition of social reality, plus court decisions that defined the child of a slave mother as a slave, soon fixed the "natural inferiority" of the Negro in the minds of white Americans. As Brown observes, "As all Negroes known to the colonists were slaves, freedmen, or the descendants of slaves, it was easy to assume that slavery was the natural and appropriate status for Negroes."[6] Thus, even after the legal condition of slavery was abolished, the idea that Negroes might be the social and political equals of white Americans had to compete with a longstanding assumption that this was unnatural. Segregation and discrimination served only to perpetuate this assumption, not to create it.

Even though its culture was beginning to be distorted by the presence of an ever-growing slave population, the South of colonial days was much less nearly solid as a region than it was to become later. For many decades slavery and the plantation system were concentrated along the Atlantic coast and there were sharp differences between the Tidewater areas and the lands of the western frontier. Frederick Jackson Turner observed:

> Through a long period of our history the "Solid South" did not exist. We must bear in mind, not only the differ-

ences between the various states of the Southern seaboard, but also the more fundamental differences between
the upcountry (the Piedmont region) and the Atlantic
Plains.[7]

The southern colonies were different from each other as
well as from the middle and northern colonies. Each had its
own government, its own crops, its own plantation system.
When the break with England came, each colony declared its
independence separately, adopted its own constitution, and
issued its own money. When the states sent delegates to the
Constitutional Convention, the southern states were not even
united on the question of slavery. The adamant defense of the
institution by delegates from South Carolina and Georgia made
compromises necessary. Delegates from the upper South questioned the value of slavery to their states and were the agents
of compromise between the North and the Deep South.
No sooner had the new nation been formed, however, than
sectional issues began to unite the southern states and set them
in conflict against other sections. Industry was beginning to
develop in the North, but the South remained an agricultural
region. Therefore the matter of tariffs became a burning issue
moving the region toward unity. The rise of the cotton culture
after the invention of the cotton gin not only served to unite
the South in defense of slavery; it served also to extend the
South and to unite the upcountry and the lowlands. John C.
Calhoun, the champion of states' rights, "represented the newer
South that cotton had created as it united the uplands and the
low country in the Carolinas and tied them in with the states
of the planting frontier."[8]
Economic dependence on cotton and slavery led to the growing conviction in the South that, whatever the evils of the
system, the slave states could not survive without it—not even
Virginia, which raised slaves mainly for export. There was still
concern about, and opposition to, slavery in the region, however; in 1827 there were 106 abolition societies in the South.
Then the intensification of the abolitionist crusade from the
North laid the foundation for a "closed society" in which
support of white supremacy became the mark of southern ortho-

doxy. The expression of antislavery sentiments was virtually proscribed in the South, and by 1837 not one of the abolition societies was left in the region. For the next quarter of a century the white people of all the southern states saw the North as a growing threat to the economy and the political power of the region.

Southern Defensiveness

Southern mythology notwithstanding, all this was only a prelude to the emergence of the defensive, minority attitude of white southerners. It has been suggested that the Old South was not solid; even its claim to be old must be questioned. C. Vann Woodward, the most perceptive interpreter of southern history, observes:

> But the Old South, so far as the Cotton Kingdom was concerned, was "old" only by courtesy, or to distinguish it from a "New South." Purely on the ground of longevity the Old South did not really last long enough in the larger part of the region to deserve the name "old." And in some states it scarcely attained a respectable middle age. By comparison with the Old South, the so-called New South, already well past the three-score-and-ten mark, is very old indeed.[9]

The Old South, slowly moving toward unity and secession from 1789 to 1861, gave birth to the Confederacy. The defeat of the Confederacy, the era of Reconstruction, and the establishment of a new basis of white supremacy gave rise to a New South, which might be called a "minority region." Although eleven southern states allied themselves in a new nation in the Confederate States of America, the South was never as united between 1861 and 1865 as romance makes it out to have been. Kentucky did not secede but tried to remain neutral in the conflict, while the eastern counties of Tennessee were dragged into the Confederacy by force. More significant was the fact that, throughout the Confederacy, States' Rights still meant the rights of *states*, not "southern rights." Jefferson

Davis was forced to contend with the governors of South Carolina and Georgia, who opposed the right of the central government to conscript their citizens for its army. There was opposition to the methods of taxation employed by the Confederate government, and Davis was an unpopular president, contending with a hostile congress from 1863 until the end of the war.

The crushing of the Confederacy created a new United States in which the old doctrine of state sovereignty was apparently a dead issue. Their dreams of political independence destroyed, the southern states became part of a reunited nation in which the reality of national sovereignty could not longer be challenged. This did not mean, however, that the cultural differences that distinguished the South from the rest of the nation no longer existed, nor that the grudges and fears that characterized the attitudes of many white southerners were dissolved in a new national consensus. The region was still agricultural and it still had a large Negro population. In addition, it had been ravaged by war and was impoverished. Forced back into a union that had not only defeated its armies but rejected its philosophy of government, it became a minority region.

The Legends of the Defeated South

Part of the minority psychology that developed can be ascribed to the experiences of defeat and of the process of reconstruction. More must be ascribed to the legends that were compounded as a salve for the wounds received in the fight for the Lost Cause.

First, there were the legends, epic in quality, that romanticized the war itself. Robert E. Lee became the Galahad of the South. This gentle, humble, and sad man was made to symbolize the alleged superiority of the gentleman-warrior of the Old South. That he was far from typical of the dashing cavalier, that as a general he was guilty of fatal tactical errors at times, that he was never a fire-eating secessionist, all were overlooked. Equally unfaithful to reality were the images of the lesser heroes of the Gray, particularly Nathan Bedford Forrest, remembered for saying "Get there fustest with the mostest" but not for permitting his troops to massacre Negro soldiers who had surrendered at Fort Pillow. Even Jefferson Davis, a thoroughly unpopular president, became a heroic figure whose birthday was honored in eight states of the South as a legal holiday. In the Deep South "Memorial Day" meant April 26, *Confederate* Memorial Day, on which for many years miniature Confederate battle flags sprouted on the graves of the martyrs to the Lost Cause. The surviving heroes (and were not they all heroes according to the legends?) marched in parades behind National Guard bands playing "Dixie," or, as their ranks began to dwindle and their stride to falter, were transported along the parade route in automobiles.

There was a counterconception, too—that of the Union army that had won the war through ungentlemanly tactics. The popular view of General U. S. Grant, perpetuated through the peculiar version of history taught in southern schools, portrayed him as a bibulous incompetent who won his battles only by overwhelming numbers and a willingness to sacrifice thousands of troops to wear down Lee's embattled army. His only redeeming feature was his graciousness to Lee at Appomattox, but his shameful record as President showed that he was still the same weak character who had resigned his regular army commission a few years after graduating from West Point. William T. Sherman was even worse; he was "the destroyer" who had burned the beautiful plantations of the Old South and allowed his drunken soldiers to steal the family silver. Part of the mythology of the conflict was the suspicion that, had the North fought a gentlemanly war, the South would have gotten at least a draw!

The second area of mythology, that pertaining to Reconstruction, also served to glorify the gentlemanly white southerner, to denigrate the "damn Yankee," and to perpetuate the stereotype of the childish, inferior black man. The heroes of the legends were kindhearted southern gentlemen, proud but gracious even in defeat, an amazing number of whom had held the rank of colonel in the late Confederate army. They honored their women, loved their children, and were deeply concerned about the plight of "their" Negroes even after freedom. Furthermore, all the freedmen except a few "bad niggers" loved them. These southern gentlemen supported the *first* Ku Klux Klan, which, according to the mythology, should in no way be confused with later versions of the Klan in which avarice and lower-class bigotry masqueraded behind the noble ideals of the original Invisible Empire. As William Randel has remarked, "Just as the Confederacy itself stimulated nostalgic regret in subsequent times, the Klan, for the same people and the same reasons, had the power to create an enduring notion of essential nobility."[10]

The South of Reconstruction times was viewed in retrospect as a living hell for decent white southerners, a hell in which illiterate blacks controlled the state governments and the mass of freedmen suffered no constraints until the Klan arose to restore order. The blacks were merely misled and exploited, however. The real villains were the Carpetbaggers, the "damn Yankees" again. It was they, with their uninhibited commercial avarice and their complete lack of familiarity with the ways of black men, who swarmed over the prostrate region to exploit the ignorance of black southerners and the helplessness of white southerners. What more proof was needed that the fear of the North that had led to secession was well founded?

A third myth that served to create a new regional unity was the myth of the antiquity of segregation as "the Southern way of life." By the time World War I had provided southern communities with a second set of heroes and white southern boys began to "kill" Germans instead of Yankees in their war games, segregation had come to seem the natural state of affairs throughout the South, even as far north as Kentucky. In *The Strange Career of Jim Crow* C. Vann Woodward exposed the fallacy of the belief that segregation laws and the "etiquette of race relations" of the early twentieth century possessed an unbroken continuity stretching back to the earliest days of the region. He shows that it was not until after the end of Reconstruction and the sanctioning of the "separate but equal" principle by the federal courts that the "era of genuine segregation" arose. He characterizes this period as "[the] era when the principle was consciously and deliberately applied to all possible areas of contact between the races, and when the code became a hard-and-fast dogma of the white race."[11]

Woodward argues that this type of comprehensive segregation did not arise and was not needed when most of the Negroes in the South were still slaves. This is not to say that before Emancipation either slaves or freedmen were treated as social equals, but the complex of laws and customs that developed after Reconstruction constituted a new system devised to keep Negro *citizens* in a position of inferiority. Woodward points out that this complex did not exist during the period of "forgotten alternatives" between 1865 and 1900.[12] The white South was divided as to how to deal with the free Negro, as the attempt to garner black votes during the Populist revolt signifies.

Between 1890 and 1896 Tom Watson of Georgia, one of the most complex figures in the history of American politics, led a revolt against the Democratic party. He called for a united front of poor farmers, black and white, to destroy the power over the South of eastern industrialists and southern landowners. In Woodward's words:

"Tom Watson was the first native white Southern leader of importance to treat the Negro's aspirations with the seriousness that human strivings deserve. For the first time in his political history the Negro was regarded neither as the incompetent ward of White Supremacy, nor as the ward of military intervention, but as an integral part of Southern society with a place in its economy."[13]

Twice Watson saw elections literally stolen from his Populist party by political chicanery that included not only ballot-box stuffing, but also the herding of black field hands to the polls by their Democratic bosses. After his defeat in 1896 as the Populist candidate for vice-president (Williams Jennings Bryan was the presidential nominee), he concluded that the Negro was an albatross around his political neck. By 1904 he was campaigning for a Democratic candidate for governor and calling for the elimination of blacks from politics. Although

he still fought vigorously for the rights of the white farmer
and laborer, in the next twenty years he became a vitriolic
propagandist against blacks, Catholics, and Jews. He was long
remembered by the lower-class white people of Georgia not as
the radical reformer who was eulogized by Eugene V. Debs,
but as the "nigger-baiter" imitated by a host of Southern
demagogues.

Just as Tom Watson turned his back on the blacks whose
cause he had once championed, the white South after 1900
sought to rebuild its political and economic fortunes by systematic and comprehensive subjugation and segregation of
the black man. Segregation was a still growing system when,
in the 1940s, federal court decisions began to destroy its legal
foundations. In the first two decades after 1900, black crafts-
men were gradually but systematically squeezed out of many
of the very trades in which they had been masters a few years
before. During the Depression the process continued; more
jobs that had traditionally been defined as "Negro jobs" were
taken over by white workers. At some point in this period, the
Negro barber who served white customers became an oddity.
New generations of white southerners who thought that letting
black hands groom them was "unsouthern" did not remember
that the valets and barbers of the Old South were black. The
intimacy-between-unequals that both slavery and the early
phases of segregation had permitted diminished as the South
became more urban and Negroes became physically more
segregated. White suburban housewives raised their children
in isolation from small black children, whereas the children's
grandparents may have played freely with black children
until puberty. Fewer whites appeared in Negro churches
(always they had been seated in a place of honor) and the
long-accepted practice of inviting black servants to share in
white family "rites of passage"—weddings and funerals—
became rare, a vestige of the day when even segregation was
less impersonal. For almost half a century the white South
had defended segregation with the saying, "Southerners love
Negroes as individuals but dislike them as a group; Yankees
love them as a group but hate them as individuals." What

truth there had been in this saying began to disappear as the South "joined the nation" in terms of urbanization and industrialization.

Growing out of the confusion and disorder of defeat and Reconstruction, segregation served to establish a new basis for white supremacy in the South. Woodward points to an equally important function that segregation served, however: "Having served as the national scapegoat in the reconciliation and reunion of North and South, the Negro was now pressed into service as a sectional scapegoat in the reconciliation of estranged white classes and the reunion of the Solid South."[14]

The political, economic, and social dominance of the slavocracy imposed a unity on the Old South of the Confederacy that the region had not possessed until the slavery controversy arose. The conviction that slavery was vital to the economy and culture of the South and that northern whites threatened the very essence of southern civilization when they attacked slavery became the basis of an orthodoxy that united, with few exceptions, all classes of ante-bellum white southerners. After 1865, the hegemony of the planter class was ended. A new structure of white classes and a new brand of politics emerged. Yet memories of the Old South lingered and, in Woodward's words: "The twilight zone that lies between living memory and written history is one of the favorite breeding places of mythology. This particular twilight zone has been especially prolific in the breeding of legend."[15]

The New South achieved its regional unity largely through the mythology of the war, of Reconstruction, and of the antiquity of segregation. The first two sets of legends glorified the white southerner and perpetuated fear and mistrust of the Yankee. The mythology of segregation enabled successive generations of white southerners to believe that the particular form that segregation took in their day constituted the historic way of the South. White supremacy through segregation became the new southern mystique. In a changing white southern society, it made all classes of white southerners equal in contrast to the Negro. In spite of its changing social structure, the white South could remain solid and could be as defensive as a genuinely persecuted minority.

New Nation, New South

The destruction of the dream of secession and the triumph of federalism created a new United States, unified by force, within which the prodigal South had to find a place. Despite nostalgia for the Old South, white southerners did not let their thoughts simply linger on the past. True, a few "unreconstructed rebels" would not accept the verdict that the Lost Cause was indeed lost. New, more influential leaders arose, however, who infused a new spirit into the region. While the Old South remained as a stimulus for fantasy, the concept of the New South became a challenge demanding realistic, future-oriented action.

William B. Hesseltine and David Smiley say of the white southerner at the end of Reconstruction, "Nostalgia beckoned him to return to the old way of life; the 'Yankee' virus of ambition and material progress urged him to create a 'New South.'"[16] In the 1880s Henry W. Grady, clearly infected by this virus, set the tone for the innumerable appeals to create a New South that would be voiced down through the years. Accepting the verdict that the South could not rebuild its old agrarian economy or that it could prosper even if it should succeed in doing so, he called on the South to catch up with the rest of the nation in industrialization and wealth. Many New Souths have been proposed since; if there is one theme that characterizes all of them, it is that of "catching up," thus revealing the defensiveness and the sense of inferiority of the loyal white southerner. Grady himself gave voice to part of this defensiveness, for as he delivered his "New South" speeches to northern audiences he reflected his conviction that the North was exploiting the South. Three-quarters of a century later white southern spokesmen would still be arguing that the region was held back in its development by the imposition of a colonial economy.

For, as seen through the eyes of some of its most loyal sons, the South, like the Negro, never seems to catch up no matter how hard it runs. Despite all the social changes that have taken place in the region, the reality of the New South is something that always remains to be achieved. Usually there is an expression of hope that this reality is something that can and will come into being, but this hope is always expressed in the context of a sober stock-taking that reveals that the South is still behind.

It has been observed that the South is "perhaps the most thoroughly interpreted part of the United States."[17] In 1936, Howard W. Odum's massive *Southern Regions of the United States* appeared as a comprehensive inventory of the condition of the South and as a challenge to the achievement of regional excellence through planning. Two years later Jonathan Daniels "discovered" his own region and found it still wanting—and still the victim of discrimination. In *A Southerner Discovers the South*, he declared, "Such a plan for a new, free, fed, housed, happy South must include not merely program at home for improvement but also program in the nation for the relinquishment of advantages elsewhere over the South."[18] In 1942 Virginius Dabney, in *Below the Potomac*, expressed the belief that a great future *awaited* the South, a future that could be built after the war against fascism abroad had been won.[19] In 1947 Odum, in *The Way of the South*, found the region coming to another epoch in its life but pointed out that there was still a great distance between "what the South has and what it wants."[20] Ironically, he quoted Walter Lippmann as having said in 1927 that the period of the eclipse of the South was over and that "from now on the South will be part of this epoch-making change" that would characterize the whole nation.[21]

By the 1960s Ralph McGill, of the Atlanta *Constitution*, had joined the company of liberal southern writers who sought to interpret the region both to its sons and to outsiders. He found a South that was becoming exciting and progressive. "There was, as 1962 ended, a picture and pattern of material progress that would have had Henry Grady dancing editorial jigs." Yet the South was still catching up. "But the Southern leadership that looked beneath the surface could see that the New South had by no means arrived. The more proper description is that of an emerging South—a South at last breaking out of the cocoon of its past."[22]

Thus there is in the thinking of many of the white people of the region the same sort of consciousness of having collectively gotten a late start that pervades the literature of the black minority in America. Something of the same desperation to catch up is also found. In a sense, the white South has been demanding "integration" for itself as vigorously as it has resisted integration for Negroes.

At the same time, urgings that the South become like the rest of the nation have been accompanied by expressions of fear of the alien. The belief that the South is different from and somehow superior to the materially richer regions has not died; warnings against the corrupting effects of outside influences, of another Yankee invasion, have cropped up in various forms.

The Industrialization of the South

By 1920 the South had forgotten its fear of blue-coated soldiers and had welcomed home a new generation of heroes who had fought side by side with Yankees in the neutral uniform of olive drab. The region seemed to be pursuing Henry Grady's dream with a passion. Towns that had been insignificant before 1861, like Birmingham and Atlanta, were becoming great industrial and commercial cities. Suddenly, out of Vanderbilt University, there came a cry of alarm in a book called *I'll Take My Stand*, written by twelve of the region's outstanding authors.[23] They called themselves "the Agrarians." Their concern and their warning have been summed up as follows:

All around them the young Southern writers saw a country doing its best to become "modern," "progressive," "up-to-date," and, as they viewed it, achieving only faddishness, unbelief, and a tawdry commercialism. In the South's eager race to emulate the rest of the country, all the things that they had been taught were good were being cast aside. Business was in the saddle; the chamber of commerce reigned.[24]

While the literature of the Agrarians may have breathed new life into southern sectionalism and contributed to the myth of the romantic past, it did not stem the tide of industrialization. The chamber of commerce continued to reign. The sort of progress that the southern chamber-of-commerce mentality proposed had a peculiarly reactionary and sectional quality, however. The appeal to new industry made by hundreds of local committees was writ large in Mississippi's "balance-agriculture-with-industry" plan, which was inaugurated during the Great Depression. The plan permitted cities to pass bond issues to finance the building of factories as a boon to new industries, and it authorized them to grant five-year tax exemptions to the companies. It was the less tangible, more subtly expressed, benefits that gave the plan its southern flavor, however. Ralph McGill has said of this subtle appeal:

> This was an invitation to employers—the good and the bad—in all regions. Both knew what [Governor White] meant. There would be no unions. And if a surplus of "native, Anglo-Saxon citizenship" was to be docile, accepting gratefully what was offered, then just how cheap could one hire a huge Negro labor force to do the common labor.[25]

As a result of this sort of appeal the South did continue to gain new industries, but they did not contribute greatly to the game of catching up. Many of them contributed little more to the economy of the states in which they located than their payrolls, and the wages shown on these payrolls lagged behind those in other regions. Often the best-paid employees, the executives and the skilled workers, were imported from other parts of the nation. A large share of the profits were distributed as dividends to stockholders living outside the South. Although local civic leaders rarely cared to make the computation, the cost of additional services provided by municipalities to tax-free industries had to be deducted from the income added to the economy of the host town.

With industry, there came inevitably another type of Yankee invasion. To the labor unions the South represented not just a new frontier, but a dire threat. Labor leaders knew that some companies moved their plants to the South in a deliberate attempt to escape the power of the unions. They knew, therefore, that the unions must follow industry even if it meant invading a region that had been traditionally hostile to them.

The price was high. Ralph McGill observed after a quarter of a century of organizational efforts: "A good many millions of dollars have been spent, a shocking amount of blood shed, and perhaps a hundred men killed, and yet only about seventeen per cent of the region's goods-producing and service workers are in unions as compared with about thirty-three per cent for the United States"[26]

Perforce, many of the labor organizers were northerners sent into the South as missionaries to southern workers, although there were notable exceptions like Lucy Randolph Mason, a daughter of one of the First Families of Virginia. The burden of proof that he was not an outsider coming to stir up trouble was on the labor organizer, however. He was often suspected of being a communist. In the South, this deadly epithet had begun to be linked up with the old label "Yankee." Although southerners had to concede that most Yankees, whatever their faults, were loyal Americans, communism was perceived as a foreign infection to which the polyglot North was susceptible and to which the patriotic, Anglo-Saxon South was immune. Would Atlanta allow the virulent *Daily Worker* to be published within its limits as did New York?

Furthermore, the fact that organized labor had at last been forced to come to grips with the problem of the unorganized Negro labor force deterred the organizers from bringing their gospel only to white southerners. Hence they were perceived as a threat to "the southern way of life." Employers fighting the unions made the most of this perceived threat. Some even made contributions to a revived Ku Klux Klan, which added "nigger-loving, communist labor organizers" to its list of targets. Here was a new breed of Carpetbaggers who sought not just to rob the South of its wealth but to steal the souls of its white people.

Stereotypes of the South

While the white South declaimed against successive waves of Yankee invaders, it also behaved like other minorities in displaying a hypersensitivity to unflattering stereotypes. This tendency was best illustrated by the storm of protest that arose when Secretary of Labor Frances Perkins suggested that Southerners needed to start wearing shoes! It mattered little that she was developing Franklin D. Roosevelt's theme that the South constituted the nation's "Economic Problem No. 1," that this theme had been suggested by the research of southern sociologists under the leadership of Howard W. Odum, and that there was a special place for the South in the economic programs of the New Deal. To brand the region as the nation's foremost economic problem was an insult to southern pride, and the suggestion that southerners did not wear shoes reflected typical Yankee ignorance. Virginius Dabney cautiously pointed to this tendency to stereotype the South when he wrote:

> True, there is a regrettable tendency on the part of some Northerners to regard nearly all Southerners as unlettered and provincial persons—the males as addicted to chewing tobacco and profanity, and as acquainted only mildly with cultural matters, and the females as semi-literate and given to petting.[27]

Ironically, some of the South's most famous sons and daughters contributed to the stereotypes to which their fellow southerners so violently objected. Erskine Caldwell, William Faulkner, Carson McCullers, Lillian Smith, Elizabeth Madox Roberts, and others wrote of the South with love but they favored a harsh, naturalistic style that laid bare the deficiencies of the region. Tobacco Road became a vividly real place to many Americans who had never set foot in the South; Jeeter Lester became the symbol of far more white southerners than ever resembled him, as real as his type was. White southerners knew that many nonsoutherners took these serious but exaggerated vignettes of life among white southerners literally. They resented those southerners who had contributed to a stereotype so unlike the romantic image of the glorious Old South.

Literary representations aside, white southerners have for years found themselves annoyed by the ignorance and, they suspect, the condescension that nonsoutherners display toward some of their cultural traits. Perhaps the foremost source of irritation is the widespread misunderstanding of how the native southerner uses the term, "You-all." That anyone should think that he is so ignorant as to use "Y'all" as a singular pronoun is insulting; the awkward and inaccurate attempts to mimic the southerner's use of the contraction are infuriating. Whether he has ever eaten them or not, the white southerner must often put up with teasing about such foods as "pot likker" (which some *Auslanders* think is alcoholic), "chit'lin's" (which millions of southerners have never tasted), and "hominy grits" (which most southerners know only as "grits," hominy being something else). Sometimes the white southerner is irritated by the obvious assumption that Negroes are treated even worse in the South than they actually are. Despite the tragic history of the crime, lynchers are no more frequent among white southerners than gangsters are among Italian-Americans.

The liberal white southerner has a special cross to bear. When he speaks with a southern accent, he is likely to be identified as an orthodox white supremacist. He is immediately overwhelmed by an unwelcome tide of sympathy for "the problem you people have in the South." This may be accompanied by an indecent exposure of northern white racial prejudices to him, as a presumptive fellow bigot. He may even find himself in the unexpected and uncomfortable position of defending the South as he tries to counter these stereotypes with a realistic analysis of the complexity of race relations in the region.

The Negro in the New South

Yet it is, in fact, the defensive self-consciousness of white southerners about matters of race that has contributed most to preserving a minority psychology in the New South. Indeed,

Henry Grady, in calling for a New South, proposed that white supremacy should be one of the foundation stones of the structure. It took a Negro southerner, Daniel C. Thompson, to point out that "Grady's New South was deformed, sickly, and stunted" because "he proposed that the structure of this New South should be forever segregated and that Negroes should be kept politically powerless at all cost."[28]

The South proceeded with much greater dispatch to build a new social structure that would "keep the Negro in his place" than to develop a prosperous industrial economy. Segregation laws, a lily-white one-party politics, and a vast differential in support for white and Negro schools, as well as the very presence of the majority of the nation's Negro citizens, made the region unique. It also made it an easy target for criticism. Even the research on racial and regional differences in intelligence tests given to soldiers during World War I succeeded, without design, in making the South its primary target. Although the analysis that the psychologist, Otto Klineberg, made of the findings showed that Negroes did not fare as well educationally as did whites in the North and that southern whites did not come off as well as northern whites, the southern Negro emerged as the most pitiable victim of palpable discrimination, and the southern white man as the chief perpetrator of the injustice. Angry southern white spokesmen drew different conclusions, however. The low test scores of Negroes proved to them that Negroes were racially inferior, but the relatively low scores of southern white soldiers did not signify that *they* might be biologically inferior. The low scores of both did show, however, that the South was a poor region and the victim of discrimination for, while southern states devoted a larger share of their income to education than did any other region, they still had less to spend on the schools.

The new breed of white southern politicians who rose to prominence after the disenfranchisement of Negroes and the defeat of Populism defended the South's most undemocratic practices against "outside interference." Like the spokesmen for slavery in ante-bellum days, they offered apologies for indefensible practices that made these practices seem like virtues. Not only did they oppose any steps to make Negro voting possible in the South; they fought desperately against a federal antilynching law. Many white southerners did not approve of the evil such a law attacked, but they were afraid to speak out. That the "Dixie demagogues" misrepresented the extent of support for their extreme positions was demonstrated by the rise of the Association of Southern Women for the Prevention of Lynching. While not supporting federal legislation to eradicate lynching, this association denounced the crime and demanded that there be an end to the practice of defending it in the name of southern womanhood.

The history of southern liberalism, from George Washington Cable to Ralph McGill, shows that the white South has never been solid in its racial attitudes. Edgar Thompson, a white southern sociologist, has identified the attitude that has come closest to unifying white southerners and that at the same time reveals their sense of being a minority:

> In all the racial strife and turmoil of today perhaps the thing that rankles and embitters most is what appears to be the bland assumption on the part of the outlanders that the natives of the Deep South, like the natives of Deep Africa, are benighted and primitive enough to be urgently in need of conversion.[29]

Serving to perpetuate this defensiveness against outside interference was the southerners' impression that the problem of race relations in the South was always being discovered anew by the outlanders. Odum said of the period of rising racial tensions during World War II:

> Once again, it was as if the rest of the Nation, in particular the publicists, the intelligentsia, and the youth of other regions had suddenly discovered the structure of the South's biracial culture. They kept saying, "What is this new thing the South is doing to the Negro? What are we going to do about the South's treatment of the Negro?" Yet, it is not surprising that the new generation of the Nation, largely ignorant of the earlier backgrounds of national development, should know little or nothing of the tragedies of the South. There grew up quickly, therefore, a remarkable concern to save the South, to free

the South, to take the occasion of war to purify American democracy.[30]

The war years were a period of tension and social change. This period followed hard on the heels of the Depression era during which the growing federal bureaucracy and the labor unions had already aroused fears of outside interference in the region. Now the South found itself host to thousands of soldiers, white and black, who had never before lived in the land of legal segregation. Some of them challenged the racial etiquette of the region. Rumor exaggerated both the number of such challenges and the violence of the natives' response to them. Defense industries springing up near southern cities, as well as in other regions, attracted enough Negro workers to put a strain on the traditional, exploitative domestic service market. Rumors of "Eleanor Clubs," organizations of Negro women, were rampant, as were stories of northern white officers' wives who offered servants "disgracefully high wages." Demands on the national front for fair employment practices, symbolized by the March on Washington Movement, were perceived as threatening a new Reconstruction. The white South rose to the defense of its "way of life," and it was excoriated in the national press for clinging to racist attitudes and customs in the midst of a war against racism. The oft-told story of German prisoners of war being fed in the dining room of a restaurant while Negro soldiers in United States uniforms were served in the kitchen captured the essence of this inconsistency.

In *Race and Rumors of Race*, Odum analyzed the variety of rumors that reflected the widespread concern that Negroes were about to get out of "their place" in the South. He pointed out that the people perceived as the chief persecutors and the prime threat to the South were once again "outsiders": "The chief blame was placed upon the small group of northern white intelligentsia and a small group of Negro agitators and not upon the great body of southern Negro leadership."[31] This great white southerner, a bitter foe of sectionalism, an incurable optimist in his hope for "regional balance," saw the South's reaction to the World War II period as a regression toward

3752690

Pol. 91

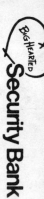

BIG HEARTED

Security Bank

DEPOSIT RECEIPT

We have today credited your checking account with the amount shown.

Checks and other items are received for deposit subject to the terms and conditions of this banks collection agreement.

When making a deposit always obtain an official receipt which must include the bank stamp.

FOR DEPOSIT TO THE ACCOUNT OF:

SBT 202

AMOUNT OF YOUR DEPOSIT

sectionalism. Under the heading, " 'North' and 'South' Again," he wrote:

> Increasingly, individuals and agencies, private and public, set themselves to the task of "making" the South change. . . . Yet the net result was an unbelievable revival of the old bitterness attached to the terms "North" and "South" what time the South resented "northern interference," and what time the North tried to coerce the South again.[32]

An indication of the resurgence of southern sectionalism was seen in the "Dixiecrat" third party movement of 1948. In 1928 an unprecedented number of white southerners had temporarily left the Democratic party to vote Republican in protest against Al Smith's Catholicism. Twenty years later a large bloc of white southerners found the Democratic regime of Harry Truman too liberal in race relations, with all its talk of FEPC, but this time they did not turn to the Republicans. They attempted to establish a *southern* party under Strom Thurmond.

This revival of sectional resentment, of minority defensiveness, was as nothing compared to the sense of discrimination and coercion that arose when the U.S. Supreme Court, in 1954, declared that school segregation was unconstitutional, *Plessy v. Ferguson* notwithstanding.

The South Rises Again

There was a desperate, back-to-the-wall quality about the Southern Resistance of the 1950s that had not been present in the earlier revivals of sectionalism. Threatened with industrialization, antilynching laws, abolition of the poll tax, destruction of the white primary, fair employment practice orders, and even the desegregation of graduate schools, conservative white southerners had sensed an impending crisis and had shouted, "These changes will lead to the destruction of the southern way of life!" Yet for half a century the doctrine of "separate but equal" had withstood all challenges and south-

ern politicians had found ways to contain the threats to segregation. Despite the cries of alarm the structure of segregation
had remained essentially strong and pervasive. With the constitutional principle established in *Plessy v. Ferguson* struck
down, however, the threatened crisis had finally arisen: Arma-
geddon was to be now. James W. Vander Zanden wrote of the
cumulative effects of social change upon the south: "Many
white Southerners would like to quarantine major change at
the Potomac. But despite their efforts a way of life is being
swept from under them—a way of life for which the race issue
has become symbolic. And it is upon the race issue they have
chosen to take their stand."[33]

A spirit similar to that which prevailed a century before, in
the decade preceding the Civil War, developed in the South.
The old, discredited theory of nullification was exhumed and
revived as the doctrine of interposition. This was the notion
that any state could interpose its sovereignty to prevent en-
forcement of a federal law until the passage of a constitutional
amendment. The Ku Klux Klan experienced another revival.
A new and more powerful resistance organization arose, the
White Citizens Council, a force more dangerous than the Klan
because it had a façade of respectability. Homage to Dixie and
the Confederate battle flag regained a significance that they
had lost over the years. In Vander Zanden's words:

> An inescapable feature of contemporary southern life
> is the linkage of the anti-integrationist movement with a
> revivalism of the symbols of the Confederacy. Southern-
> ism has evolved as a cult, as a political creed in much the
> fashion of communism, socialism, and fascism. Through
> the years the South has become for many Southerners
> something more than a matter of geography. It has become
> an object of pride, patriotism, and identification.[34]

The white South was once again an embattled minority,
with the forces of the Supreme Court, the NAACP, northern
liberalism, and "Yankee ignorance" arrayed against it. Many
astute southern lawyers recognized that the Supreme Court
would not reverse itself and that the South would have to live
with the consequences of the Brown decision. Nevertheless

there was a widespread faith that the South could somehow repel this attack, even though it had failed in 1865.

Let it be clear: white southern attitudes were not uniform at any time during the crisis of desegregation. Research done by Melvin Tumin in the years immediately following the 1954 decision showed that a range of "readiness and resistance to desegregation" existed among white southerners, readiness being correlated with education and youth.[35] Ten years later James Prothro and Donald Matthews concluded, "Education decreases dedication to strict segregation, but extremely high levels of education are apparently necessary to produce actual acceptance of integration."[36] They concluded, however, that the previously identified relationship between youth and readiness for desegregation was not holding up: "If the young adults of the South represent the hope of the future, they may be the hope of the strict segregationists rather than of anyone else."[37] In seeking to explain this finding, they observed of white southerners who were between the ages of 21 and 29 in 1965:

> These people were between the ages of 14 and 22 at the time of the Supreme Court's school-desegregation decision in 1954. Since the "black Monday" of that decision, white youths in the South may have been subjected to a more concentrated indoctrination in the merits of segregation.[38]

Just as the slavery controversy of the nineteenth century stifled abolitionist sentiment and produced a southern orthodoxy in support of slavery, the desegregation crisis generated a new orthodoxy and created what James W. Silver called "the closed society."[39] Although Silver wrote of Mississippi, the hardest of the hard-core states, countless communities from northern Virginia to the keys of Florida experienced a closure of democratic debate that made advocacy of integration as a virtue foolhardy and acceptance of it as a necessity dangerous.

The prediction of radical segregationists that it would take bayonets to force integration on the South became a self-fulfilling prophecy. The South once again saw federal troops bivouacked in some of its communities. It also saw violence in its streets, although this violence was nearly always perpetrated against nonviolent demonstrators by modern "Confederates" in civilian clothes or policemen's uniforms. It experienced a new style of invasion, one by newspapermen and television cameramen who made headline stories of the trials and tribulations of southern communities. In such communities only a handful of the most liberal white southerners failed to share the feeling of hurt that, no matter how badly some of their fellow citizens had behaved, the press had failed to tell the whole story and had made white southerners look worse than they really were. Once more the old resentment against the stereotyping of the white southerner by Yankees was aroused. Again the source of the region's troubles was perceived to be "the outsider." In speaking of the sit-ins Prothro and Matthews observe:

> To miss the point of these dramatic events so completely requires powerful psychological defenses. White southerners—especially the segregationists and the moderates—apparently had such defenses. The major one was the belief that the sit-ins were the result of "outside agitation" rather than of genuine discontent over racial conditions; about half the explanations offered for the sit-ins by white segregationists and moderates and over a third of those offered by white integrationists were along these lines. . . .
>
> Next to the NAACP and the communists, northerners were the favorite culprits.[40]

In 1924 Herbert A. Miller coined the phrase "oppression psychosis" to describe a common reaction of members of minority groups to their status. However much discrimination and persecution may exist, the victims are hypersensitive and thus ready to perceive even more than actually exists. The white South has been stereotyped and, as a defeated region, it was subjected to deliberate punishment by the Radical Republicans during Reconstruction. Whether the severity of its punishment was enough to warrant calling it a "minority region" or not, it has reacted as if it were a persecuted minority. The persistence of the belief that unwelcome changes are the result of outside agitation has blinded a large proportion of its white citizenry to the faults of the region and to the discontent of black southerners. This belief has served as the justification for adamant resistance to change that has deepened, not alleviated, the most recent crisis.

In a way, however, the South may have begun to get its revenge on the North through the very adamance of its resistance during the decade following the 1954 Supreme Court decision. Pushing both the Negro protest movement and the federal government toward increasingly drastic measures for effecting social change, white southerners saw themselves joined by strange new allies. The black revolution spread to the North and began to develop a separatist theme that put black militants in the ironic position of denouncing integration, although for very different reasons than those that had motivated white southerners a decade earlier. Both black protestors and federal bureaucrats began to discover discrimination by school boards, policemen, employers, and realtors outside the South, lending credence to the old southern plea that criticism of the South for its racial practices was a case of "the pot calling the kettle black." According to public opinion polls, a large number of white people outside the South began to feel that there was discrimination *in favor of* Negroes.

For the first time since Lee had marched towards Gettysburg and defeat, there was a southern counterinvasion. In 1968 George Wallace of Alabama, "the heart of Dixie" according to automobile license plates, ran for president as a third party candidate with support not only in the South but in the North and West. To his southern supporters he stood as a symbol of traditional "southern rights"; outside the South, he was a symbol of "white rights" and "law and order."

The white South did not succeed in preserving segregation unblemished; it accommodated to change by inventing "tokenism." The degree of defeat involved in this compromise did not, however, serve to discourage the minority-like belief that the region had been treated unjustly. Instead, the polarization of the whole nation on the issue of race revived the hope that, as outsiders began to understand Negro-white relations the way white southerners did, the historic stance of the South would be vindicated.

From the days of the tariff controversy through the era of resistance to desegregation the regional orthodoxy has fostered the belief among white southerners that they are a mistreated minority. Ever ready to see evidence of exploitation, misunderstanding, stereotyping, and scapegoating, constantly driven by the need to achieve regional equality that always seems just beyond their grasp, loyal sons of the white South yet cling to the belief that there is some mystical superiority in "the southern way of life." That this way of life defies definition and is interpreted as having as its essence such contradictory qualities as intractable white supremacy and an ineffable graciousness in human relations reflects the fact that, despite the pervasiveness of "southernism," white southerners are a heterogeneous people.

Notes

1 Rupert B. Vance, *All These People* (Chapel Hill: The University of North Carolina Press, 1945), pp. 15–16.

2 Howard W. Odum, *Southern Regions of the United States* (Chapel Hill: The University of North Carolina Press, 1936), p. 475.

3 W. J. Cash, *The Mind of the South* (New York: Knopf, 1941).

4 For a fuller discussion of these factors, see Ina C. Brown, *Race Relations in a Democracy* (New York: Harper & Brothers, 1949), pp. 56–59.

5 *Ibid.*, p. 58.

6 *Ibid.*, p. 57.

7 Frederick J. Turner, *The Significance of Sections in American History* (New York: Holt, 1932), p. 12.

8 William B. Hesseltine and David L. Smiley, *The South in American History*, 2nd ed. (Englewood Cliffs, N.J.: Prentice-Hall, 1960), p. 130.

9 C. Vann Woodward, *The Strange Career of Jim Crow* (New York: Oxford University Press, 1957), pp. 4–5.

10 William P. Randel, *The Ku Klux Klan* (Philadelphia: Chilton, 1965), p. 7.

11 Woodward, *op. cit.*, p. xvii.

12 *Ibid.*, chap. I.

[13] C. Vann Woodward, *Tom Watson: Agrarian Rebel* (New York: Macmillan, 1938), p. 221.

[14] Woodward, *The Strange Career of Jim Crow, op. cit.*, p. 65.

[15] *Ibid.*, p. viii.

[16] Hesseltine and Smiley, *op. cit.*, p. 390.

[17] Dewey W. Grantham (ed.), *The South and the Sectional Image* (New York: Harper & Row, 1967), p. 4.

[18] Jonathan Daniels, *A Southerner Discovers the South* (New York: Macmillan, 1938), p. 344.

[19] Virginius Dabney, *Below the Potomac* (New York: Appleton-Century, 1942), p. 315.

[20] Howard W. Odum, *The Way of the South* (New York: Macmillan, 1947), p. 264.

[21] *Ibid.*, p. 267.

[22] Ralph McGill, *The South and the Southerner* (Boston: Little, Brown, 1964), p. 208.

[23] John C. Ransom *et al.*, *I'll Take My Stand* (New York: Harper and Brothers, 1930).

[24] Louis D. Rubin, Jr., "Regionalism and the Southern Literary Renascence," in Grantham, *op. cit.*, p. 54.

[25] McGill, *op. cit.*, p. 194.

[26] *Ibid.*, p. 199.

[27] Dabney, *op. cit.*, p. 14.

[28] Daniel C. Thompson, "The New South," *Journal of Social Issues,* 12 (January 1966), 7.

[29] Edgar T. Thompson, "The South in Old and New Contexts," in John C. McKinney and Edgar T. Thompson (eds.), *The South in Continuity and Change* (Durham, N.C.: The Duke University Press, 1965), p. 467.

[30] Howard W. Odum, *Race and Rumors of Race* (Chapel Hill: The University of North Carolina Press, 1943), p. 15.

[31] *Ibid.*, p. 151.

[32] Odum, *The Way of the South, op. cit.*, p. 232.

[33] James W. Vander Zanden, *Race Relations in Transition* (New York: Random House, 1965), p. 21.

[34] *Ibid.*

[35] Melvin M. Tumin, *Desegregation: Resistance and Readiness* (Princeton, N.J.: Princeton University Press, 1958).

[36] Donald R. Matthews and James W. Prothro, *Negroes and the New Southern Politics* (New York: Harcourt, Brace & World, 1966), p. 343.

[37] *Ibid.*, p. 349

[38] *Ibid.*, p. 350.

[39] James W. Silver, *Mississippi: The Closed Society* (New York: Harcourt, Brace & World, 1964).

[40] Matthews and Prothro, *op. cit.*, p. 43.

Chapter 3 ◉ Southerners: Rich, Poor, White, Black

The people of the United States have long prided themselves on the notion that their nation has been throughout its history a symbol of equality, opportunity, and freedom. Although social classes have always been identifiable in the society, the idea of entrenched and, particularly, hereditary privilege has been repugnant to the national ideals.

The South, despite the fact that it was the fountainhead of Jeffersonian and Jacksonian democracy, has been a discordant symbol of an aristocratic spirit developed and cherished throughout much of the region's history. This tradition encompassed not only the racial superiority of whites over blacks but extended even to a hierarchy of white people. It is true that the idea of southern aristocracy has always included a large component of myth, and that in recent years the class that most prided itself on its "good breeding" has been largely submerged as the population of the region has changed. Yet the aristocratic tradition remains a background against which the changing social structure must be viewed.

White southerners do not look back to the frontier days, to the times that produced Andrew Jackson, for their conception of the ideal class structure. They look instead to the Golden Age of the ante-bellum period, failing to recognize how few of their ancestors were likely to have enjoyed its luxuries. During this time "the small class of slaveowning planters, together with the wealthier urban merchants, bankers, and lawyers, formed quite definitely the ruling class."[1] There was a somewhat larger upper middle class of small planters, commercial farmers, and lesser merchants and professionals.[2] The largest segment of the white population consisted of yeoman farmers who owned no slaves or only one or two, independent white artisans, and highlanders. The true under class of the Old South included the landless, unskilled "po' whites," scorned by other white southerners and even by the black slaves.

The slave population provided the foundation of this system, a system that made the large planter the symbol of success. The blacks constituted the wealth that, along with the land, made possible the existence of the planter aristocracy. Justification of black slavery contributed a major part to the development of an antidemocratic ideology in the Old South. "As the planter class felt an ever-mounting need to justify slavery, it tended to turn to a philosophy of caste in which slavery was divinely ordained and every white man also had his place."[3]

Views differ as to the extent to which the Old South did develop a genuine aristocracy. W. J. Cash debunked the aristocratic pretensions of the planter class, arguing that its members created a myth of Cavalier ancestry in order to obscure their plebeian origins.[4] Rudolph Heberle suggests that the planters were developing the traits of a true aristocracy and "an emergent aristocratic group consciousness indicated by the formulation of ideologies opposed to democratic ideals as well as to the social ethics of the bourgeois entrepreneur."[5] These distinctions are for academicians to debate, however. The popular, romantic image of the ante-bellum South exaggerates both the size and the antiquity of the class of "old southern families" and "southern gentlemen," just as romanticism has staffed the Confederate Army with an unwieldy number of generals and colonels. The white-columned mansions that still dot the region conjure up visions of a Camelot such as could not be imagined anywhere else in America. This myth has cast a long shadow over the evolving class structure of the South.

The New Middle Class and the Aristocratic Tradition

Writing in 1939, Hortense Powdermaker observed of a Mississippi town that the middle class of whites had grown in numbers and power at the expense of the large plantation owners. She added, however:

In our community their sway is evident and unquestioned. It is evident, too, that they in turn are dominated by vestiges of the past: by their reverence for the great tradition of the South, by the insecurities attendant upon new and unaccustomed powers, by the fears and conflicts of the interracial situation.[6]

Powdermaker observed also a desire on the part of the new ruling class to see themselves as lineal descendants of the old aristocracy.

In this connection it is significant that the majority of the Whites in Cottonville do not admit to being middle class as readily as would a similar group in Ohio or Indiana. Indeed, almost every Mississippian will give one to understand that he is descended from a family of high estate and rank.[7]

The Civil War and Reconstruction led to drastic changes in the social structure of the South. The planter class had been dethroned. The fact that the planters had fallen from power did not mean, however, that as a class they had been liquidated or exiled. Although it was impoverished and stripped of its political power, this class survived as a link with the old order. For one thing, many of the plantations were preserved because Reconstruction included no radical program of land redistribution. Tenant farmers and sharecroppers, both black and white, replaced the slaves. The white tenants and sharecroppers became a new class between 1865 and the beginning of the Great Depression. At the same time, there was a change in the composition of the planter class. "Among the planters there emerged a large proportion of 'new men' coming up from the ranks of overseers and from the farmer classes. On the other hand, many of the old planter families, having lost slaves and other capital, turned to business and the professions."[8]

The onset of a new era of industrialization and urbanization was accompanied by the growth of a commercial and manufacturing class in the towns and cities. This class supplied the still-dominant agricultural sector of the economy and operated the new industries, particularly cotton mills. A new class of white industrial laborers emerged in the mill towns of the region. By 1900 there were 416 cotton mills in the South, almost half of the national total. The Carolinas led in cotton manufacturing. Between 1880 and 1900 lumbering developed as an industry in the lower South, and coal and iron mining became important in the Appalachian mountains from Virginia to Alabama. The Duke family of North Carolina took the lead in building an empire in the tobacco industry, which was new to the nation as well as to the South. Employers in all of these mines and mills looked primarily to poverty-stricken rural whites as a source of cheap, tractable labor.[9]

As Powdermaker's comments suggest, it was the new, urban middle class that became the center of power, replacing the planter aristocracy. Yet, no matter how little justification there was for it, there was a sense of continuity with the past. There had been no internal revolution to overthrow the planter class, even though the Populist revolt had represented a reaction to their attempt to regain political power. It was the Yankee invasion that had toppled them from the throne. Divested of their wealth and power, replaced by new landowners, they remained heroes. William H. Nicholls points out that while most of the new middle class of the postwar South were born of parents who had not been slaveholders, they "usually found it politic to bring into their organizations men of authentic planter origin, whose names brought the prestige of aristocratic lineage or glorious war records."[10] The concept of the southern gentleman remained alive even in an increasingly urban milieu, among a new bourgeoisie of nonaristocratic, sometimes nonsouthern lineage.

The Decline of Agrarian Dominance

To understand the amazing endurance of what was from the start a dubious tradition of aristocracy, one must remember that the urbanization and industrialization of the South developed relatively slowly. Until 1930 and almost until 1940 the South remained a predominantly agricultural region. The relatively progressive spirit of the urban middle class still had to compete with the conservatism of the rural population. Change was often stifled by rural-dominated legislatures. Moreover, the nature of southern industry, manifested in relatively low wages for the average industrial worker, preserved a sense of a status society that was conducive to lingering notions of aristocracy. Perhaps one reason the concept of "po' white trash" survived so long was that there were so many white southerners who were visibly poor even though they might be employed. In a textile town studied by Kenneth Morland the workers had been called "cotton mill trash" by the townspeople when the mills were new.[11] Blacks were not the only southerners who were segregated; company-owned "mill villages" were highly visible sections of many growing southern cities.

Many observers have agreed that until 1930 the social structure and the culture of the South strongly reflected the influence of the older plantation economy. The devotion of white southerners to a segregated biracial system is often identified as the primary deterrent to rapid change. William Nicholls, an economist, attaches equal significance to the continued division of southern society into separate urban and rural compartments.[12] According to his interpretation, the rural segment retained a broad lower class base, particularly in the black belt. (See Appendix, Table 4, for ranks of southern states by percent urban, 1910 and 1960.) This, in turn, limited the relative size and importance of the new middle class in the urban segment because of the constant flow of unskilled, impoverished farm workers into the growing cities. Nicholls argues that the rural-urban barrier, which kept large numbers of whites as well as blacks in a low-income status, was more formidable than the race barrier in slowing the pace of social change.

A sociologist, Leonard Reissman, characterizes the persistence of the social structure in these words:

As late as 1930 the South could be characterized as a regional society built upon aristocratic domination, aristocratic sentiments, and aristocratic traditions. The plantation and magnolia image of the antebellum South was somewhat tarnished as Tennessee Williams has informed us repeatedly, but aristocratic traditions did not die easily.

The South's stratification structure was steeply pyramidal: a small, land-owning and commercial elite at the top; a relatively small middle class of professionals, managers and public officials; a large segment including the small farmers, tenant farmers, and the urban poor; and finally, the whole of this structure resting upon the bulk of the Negro population bound to agriculture. The caste barrier separated Negro from white, and just as surely, the aristocratic barrier separated the elite from all others . . . Whatever mobility there was seemed to be confined largely to the cities, which were not yet sufficiently dynamic to support any widespread upward mobility.[13]

It was not influences originating within the region that finally brought about more drastic changes in the social structure of the South. It was the Great Depression of the 1930s and the involvement of the nation in World War II that speeded up change. These two forces, with their roots in the world situation, induced changes in the population and the culture that finally made the South an urban region and broke the grip of the aristocratic tradition. (See Appendix, Table 5, for percent of southern population classified as urban, 1790–1960.)

Except for brief periods of net migration to farms in 1932 and immediately after World War II, migration from the rural South to urban places in both the South and the North was continuous after 1920. Yet when Franklin D. Roosevelt was elected president in 1932, the South's agricultural economy was not adequately supporting the number of people who still remained on the land. The federal policy implemented by the Agricultural Adjustment Administration changed southern agriculture in a way that soil erosion and the boll weevil had not done. Subsidized acreage reduction made tenants and sharecroppers surplus to an extent never before realized, since landlords received subsidies for removing land from cultivation. This program placed a premium on efficiency in working the land, thus constituting a powerful stimulus for reducing the number of tenants and for adopting mechanization. While the agricultural relief measures saved the farm owners from economic ruin, they forced thousands of tenants and sharecroppers to seek employment in the urban, industrial sector of the economy.[14]

Long after the end of the New Deal and its emergency measures the mechanization of farming continued to reduce the need for agricultural workers in the South. Although it continued to be the most agricultural, least industrialized region, the South became more like the rest of the nation. By 1960 only about 10 percent of southern workers were employed in agriculture, forestry and fishing, compared with 6.7 percent in the country as a whole. The region still lagged in employment in manufacturing, with only 21.3 percent of its workers in manufacturing as compared with 27.1 percent in the nation as a whole.[15]

The Effects of Urbanization

As workers left the land, southern cities grew, so that one could begin to speak realistically of metropolitan areas in the South resembles the national pattern. . . . The metropolitan conurbations and two lesser metropolitan complexes that, in 1960, included almost 40 percent of the total population of the South (he included the Southwest).[16] The five conurbations centered on: (1) Houston and New Orleans; (2) the Miami and Tampa areas of South Florida; (3) Atlanta; (4) Dallas and Fort Worth; and (5) the Piedmont region of the Carolinas. He saw smaller metropolitan complexes developing around Shreveport, Louisiana, and the Nashville-Memphis area of Tennessee. Only the states of Mississippi and Arkansas appeared to be largely bypassed by this process of metropolitization. Reissman observes:

> The metropolitan pattern that has emerged in the South resembles the national pattern. . . . The metropolitan conurbations in the South mean the end of the region as a homogeneous unity and the creation of a new alignment in which the older boundaries and older loyalties have less functional meaning.[17]

As urbanization has taken place, what has happened to the "steeply pyramidal stratification structure"? The United States

Census for 1960 offers a measure of socioeconomic status not available in previous censuses. This is a socioeconomic status score, based on a combination of measures of income, occupation, and education. Comparison of these scores not only reflects the relative socioeconomic status of people living in different regions but also gives some indication of the class structure. The data show that although the South may have changed a great deal, it is still different.

First of all, a higher proportion of people are lower class in the South than in the rest of the nation. This does not result solely from the presence of the black poor. The median socioeconomic status score for whites in the United States as a whole was 54.6. While the corresponding scores for whites in each of the other regions exceeded this score, the median score for white southerners was 49.1.

If we divide the white population into quartiles according to the percentage with "high," "upper middle," "lower middle," and "low" scores, we find evidence of lingering traces of the older class structure in the South. Whites throughout the nation and in the South (as that region is defined by the U.S. Census) are distributed as shown below:

Socioeconomic Status of White Population, 1960

(Percent Distribution)

	SES SCORES	U.S.	SOUTH
High	(75–99)	20.0	16.8
Upper-Middle	(50–74)	37.3	31.9
Lower-Middle	(25–49)	29.9	32.0
Low	(0 –24)	12.9	19.2

SOURCE: Based on *United States Census of Population,* 1960, *Subject Reports, Socioeconomic Status,* Final Report PC(2)-SC, Table 2.

Although the differences are small, the upper class among white southerners, according to this crude measure, is still relatively small and the lower class disproportionately large. The middle class tends to be somewhat more "lower-middle" than does the national middle class.

A far greater proportion of the lower-middle-class and lower-class white southerners now live in cities. Many of them have emigrated from farms and small towns within the region. They no longer live in the shadow either of the plantation or the county courthouse, nor do they enjoy an easy camaradarie with rural political oligarchs. Like many other white southerners of all classes, they have sometimes voted Republican and have lost their traditional faith in the Democratic party. They have seen the symbol of their social superiority to blacks, legal segregation, shattered, and in some cases they find themselves competing with black southerners for jobs. Their faith in the durability of the southern way of life has been destroyed.

A political scientist, Charles O. Lerche, Jr., contends that it is the disruption of the familiar environment of so many rural, lower-class white southerners by the urbanization of the South that is the chief source of recent political changes in the region. If his conclusions are valid, the powerful influence of the past will still be felt as the transition of the region into an urban, industrial society continues. In Lerche's words:

> Southern protest, whatever its immediate referents in any particular place, grows ultimately from the almost inchoate resentments of the back-country farmer or small towner (who may or may not have already moved to the city) in revolt against a changing society that denies him his old place but fails to provide a new and satisfying one.[18]

The old, pseudoaristocratic tradition of the South has been all but swept away by urbanization. The one-party system has been destroyed, and black voters have become a new and important force in politics. Differences between the "hard core" or Deep South states of Alabama, Georgia, Louisiana, Mississippi, and South Carolina and the other southern states are becoming more evident, as are differences between metropolitan areas and the hinterlands. Southern white political conservatism, which is largely rooted in the class structure of the region, has not yet disappeared, however.

Southern Conservatism, New Style

Southern demagogues, albeit of a new variety, continue to arise. Today they may be Republicans or Democrats, or they may declare their independence of both major parties. They no longer base their campaigns crudely and blatantly on "nigger-baiting," but they still appeal in subtle but transparent ways to the sentiment of white supremacy. Federal interference, public "giveaway programs," "crime in the streets," student revolts, "softness toward communism," and "law and order" are national issues, not peculiarly southern ones. The clever southern white politician can use these issues to mask his appeal to the racist sentiments of his constituency even as he proclaims his concern for the welfare of black voters. Now, however, white southern conservatives find it easier to join forces with conservative voters in other parts of the nation. The historic congressional alliance of southern Democrats and conservative Republicans now has its counterpart at the polls in the South. Furthermore, the malaise that many white southerners are experiencing in the face of rapid social change has its counterpart in the deep concern for law and order expressed by many white voters outside the South. White southern conservatism may prove to be only one component of a national movement that will go beyond conservatism to outright reaction.

The prospects for rapid change in the South have been questioned by Edwin M. Yoder in a commentary on "W. J. Cash After a Quarter of a Century." Yoder asks, "Has the essential behavior of the South as Cash described it changed radically in the last quarter-century?" His answer:

> On the whole the answer seems to me No—notwithstanding obvious economic and social modifications that are often heralded today, as in the 1890's, as constituting a "New" South. In truth "the mind of the South" seems today to defy the impersonal forces. When you put aside the spread of television sets, the advent of jet air travel, the large cash incomes (all consistent with national developments), you are left with a mental pattern familiar

to Cash: the race picture, though increasingly subject to
federal legal pressure, is mostly as Cash saw it—status
politics still intact. The South is still given, more than
any single identifiable region, to unholy repressions of
wrong thinking.[19]

As if documenting Yoder's conclusion, a southern newspaper editor wrote during the 1968 presidential campaign:

> I sense an intimidation factor in this presidential cam-
> paign that is making the people more guarded than usual
> in showing their preferences.
> It may be only indecision, perhaps some indifference,
> but it doesn't seem that our Southern voters particularly
> are whooping it up for their candidates unless they are
> George Wallace supporters, and even some of them may
> be sitting quietly. . . . On a tour through five states . . .
> the first observation is that there are almost no bumper
> strips on Southern automobiles except those proclaiming
> support for George Wallace.[20]

As recently as 1963 James W. Silver wrote of Mississippi as
"The Closed Society."[21] While no entire state, except perhaps
Alabama, has matched Mississippi in the repression of dissent,
there have been many communities in other southern states
that have been part of the Closed Society.

The South changes—a New South is always emerging and
is repeatedly acclaimed by loyal, optimistic sons of the region.
Technology expands, the landscape is reshaped, the external
behavior of the people violates many of the old customs, but
the idea of the South as essentially different survives. Traditions of status, of individualism, of reverence for the past, as
well as those of friendliness and easy living, are cherished by
enough white southerners to maintain continuity with the past
and to keep alive the idea of "the southerner." It remains to be
seen how long a period of transition will be required for the
emergence of a truly "new" South, a South that has indeed
"joined the rest of the nation." Even then, just what joining
the rest of the nation may signify in terms of democracy is
uncertain. Despite drastic changes in the outward appearance
of race relations and in the rhetoric of southern politicians,

the spirit of white supremacy still retains much of its vitality. At the same time, conservative white southerners are finding that they have many allies in the lily-white suburbs of the North and West.

Black Southerners

The onslaught of the civil rights movement evoked from white southerners many expressions that became stereotyped responses to the racial crisis. "We won't have any trouble here —we have a good class of colored people!" "Our Negroes are happy—these outsiders should leave them alone." "We were making real progress until the Supreme Court interfered." Also heard was another expression that was less optimistic but had deeper significance: "I always thought I understood our colored people but now I feel like I never knew them at all."

Black southerners have always been a familiar, seemingly essential part of the background of the white southerner's existence. By the same token, the South has always exercised a pervasive influence on the lives of black Americans wherever they may live. Collectively, blacks have roots in the South that reach as deep as those of any white southerner. There are few blacks in the United States who cannot trace their ancestry to a slave family in the South, and most can find a white southerner in their family trees. The vast majority of the inhabitants of black ghettos in northern and western states are migrants or the children of migrants from the South. The accents heard in the ghettos are predominantly southern. Soul food, whether served in Harlem, Watts, or Atlanta, originated in the rural South. The educational problems of black children, wherever they are, must be ascribed in part to the historic deficiencies of segregated southern schools. The force of national legislation that affects the lives of black citizens everywhere is still tempered by the maneuverings of white southern congressmen and senators. Even the most militant black nationalists, the self-proclaimed government-in-exile of the Republic of New Africa, claim five states of the Deep South (South Carolina, Georgia, Alabama, Mississippi, and Louisiana) as the historic homeland of all black Americans. They propose that the heartland of Dixie become the exclusive preserve of Afro-Americans rather than that the South or the nation become integrated.

Emancipation and the granting of full citizenship rights to black Americans held the promise of making the black southerner an equal partner in the life of the South, but disenfranchisement and segregation pushed him into the background again. Even after they lost the Civil War, white southerners were able to forestall for almost another century radical changes in the biracial society. Like an embattled minority they fought all "outside" attempts to change the system. John Hope Franklin has put it this way:

> The heavy hand of history has been a powerful force in the maintenance of a segregated society and, conversely, in the resistance to change. Americans, especially Southerners, whose devotion to the past is unmatched by that of any others, have summoned history to support their arguments that age-old practices and institutions cannot be changed overnight, that social practices cannot be changed by legislation. Southerners have argued that desegregation would break down long-established customs and bring instability to a social order that, if left alone, would have no serious racial or social disorders. After all, Southern whites "know" Negroes; and their knowledge has come from many generations of intimate association and observation, they insist.[22]

There were, it is true, white southern voices calling for change, as represented by the Association of Southern Women for the Prevention of Lynching, the Commission on Interracial Cooperation, and the Southern Regional Council. These all played a part in softening the impact of white dominance on black southerners, but none were able to challenge segregation effectively; until after mid-century the color line remained essentially unchanged. During the tumultuous decade between the Supreme Court school desegregation decision of 1954 and the passage of the 1964 Civil Rights Law, however, it became obvious that the racial order based on legal segregation was doomed.

The most obvious and oft-reviewed forces that induced change in the racial order were the pressures from outside the South that southerners, whether white or black, had little part in initiating. Despite their impotence during the long period of accommodation following the end of Reconstruction, black southerners did contribute indirectly and, finally, directly to changing the racial order. Gradually and unobtrusively they came to be more an urban people and less a rural peasantry in the South itself. More spectacularly, they left the South in growing numbers, and it can be safely predicted that by 1970 as many black Americans will live outside the South as live in it. Finally, in the civil rights movement they did seize the initiative in forcing change on the South.

Migration to Southern Cities

The immensity of the impact of the migration of black southerners to cities of the North and West has drawn attention from the fact that a large number were sharing significantly in the urbanization of the South itself. By 1960, 58.5 percent of the black population of the South was classified as urban. Many of these people, like their brothers who had migrated to the North, were crowding into the central cities of southern metropolitan areas. Between 1950 and 1960 the proportion of nonwhites in the central portions of the largest cities in the South grew, just as it did in the cities of other regions. The densely populated, expanding black ghetto became part of the southern scene.

The urbanization of the black southern population and the escape of so many blacks from the repressive milieu of the small town did not mean that the South had entered a new era of harmonious, egalitarian race relations. That the quality of race relations was changing was clear to all, white or black. What these changes might portend for the welfare of black southerners and the racial attitudes of white southerners remains far from clear.

Black southerners, even in the cities, remained an economically underprivileged class to an even greater extent than did urban blacks in other regions. In the central cities of the South, 86.3 percent of blacks were found to have socioeconomic scores of less than 50 by the 1960 census, as compared with 77.7 percent of blacks living in central cities in the United States as a whole. Of the black families living in central cities in the South, 83.1 percent reported annual incomes of less than $3,000.[23] One study of selected southern cities suggested that whereas the urban black southerner is wealthier in absolute terms than his rural counterpart, "he becomes less equal in relative terms to the white population around him in the indices of education, occupation, and for the most part, income."[24] According to this study, made in 1967, a smaller proportion of black southerners were sharecroppers or hired hands on southern farms than in the past but most were still relatively unskilled, poorly educated, and, above all, poor.

Speaking of New Orleans, the city with the largest concentration of blacks in the South, Daniel Thompson has pointed out that the median income of blacks was only about 65 percent that of whites in 1960; it had been almost 60 percent in 1940. Thompson's description of how slowly this gap is being narrowed dramatizes the plight of the black southerner who seeks to improve his fortunes by cityward migration in the region:

> The vast majority of Negroes in New Orleans, about 85 per cent, may be classified as blue-collar workers. (Only about 35 per cent of white workers may be so classified.) About half of the Negro workers in this category may be designated as menial laborers. They hold what has been traditionally considered "Negro jobs"— jobs that pay the lowest wages and provide the least security.[25]

Still deprived relative to whites in the urbanized South, the black southerner finds himself isolated from them in a new way. His isolation becomes more physical and impersonal. Personal, even friendly, contacts with whites were more frequent in the small town even though these contacts were circumscribed by the etiquette of race relations. Philip Hauser's inquiry into the effects of the urbanization of black Americans in the half-century following 1910 applies as well to the South as to other regions:

> Thus, it may be argued that the cataclysmic social upheaval occasioned by the two world wars generated both opportunity for and barriers to integration. On the one hand, it removed Negroes from their segregation in the rural South which had precluded meaningful contact with white society and had barred their assimilation into American society. On the other hand, it poured so large a Negro population into the cities, and especially the large cities, over so short a period of time that it made the Negro in-migratory stream relatively unassimilable—economically, socially, and politically. It remains to be seen whether this is a relatively short-term phenomenon or whether, given their huge enclaves in the cities, Negroes have been freed from their segregation and isolation in the rural slum South only to be thrust into a new form of segregation and isolation in the urban slum in the North, West, and South.[26]

This increased segregation and isolation, in combination with the intervention of outside pressures, has had another important consequence for black southerners. When, through federal voting rights laws and the "one man, one vote" decisions of the Supreme Court, the political stranglehold of rural white voters was broken, black southerners found themselves able to elect some of their own group to state and local offices. In December 1968, the Southern Regional Council sponsored an unprecedented "Southwide Conference of Black Elected Officials." Although the 1965 federal Voting Rights Law was only three years old at the time the conference was planned, there were already 385 black elected officials in the region. Some were, of course, local officers elected in predominantly black, rural counties, such as the black sheriff of Macon County, Alabama. Black mayors—Charles Evers of Fayette, Mississippi, and Howard Lee, of Chapel Hill, North Carolina —had not yet been elected in southern communities. The keynote speaker for the conference was the symbol of the new, urban, black South—Julian Bond, member of the Georgia legislature, now nationally known for his role at the 1968 Democratic national convention. Bond owed his seat in the legislature to the fact that blacks constituted the overwhelming majority of voters in his district in Atlanta.

Given the development of a new mood of militance, the sheer numbers of black southerners concentrated in urban ghettos came to constitute the greatest threat to the traditional racial order. "The most obvious implication for Negroes of the urbanization of the South is that they escape the heavy, albeit sometimes benign, hand of white paternalism. In the areas of Negro concentration in the central city they escape not only the hand but the eye of the white man."[27] In the isolated world of the ghetto, protest groups have been able to develop, formulate strategy, mobilize forces, and launch attacks on segregation and discrimination with greater impunity than they could in small towns. At first these militant groups marched forth to stage nonviolent sit-ins or to man picket lines. Peaceful demonstrators endured the blows of counter-demonstrators and the police. Sometimes violence or threats of violence followed them into the black community. Homes were fired into and churches were bombed. As the black revolution turned from nonviolence to defensive violence, the black sections of southern communities took on a new and menacing character for white southerners. Traditionally the white southerner had little fear of going into "niggertown." His confidence in black fear of white retaliation for violence against any member of the master race provided him with an invisible armor. Today this sense of security is rapidly disappearing. Numerous blacks have met white violence with their own. In 1960, five years before the Watts insurrection, blacks in Jacksonville, Florida, had vented their wrath at white injustice in a "property riot" and had attacked whites who came into the ghetto during the disorder. During the "long, hot summers" of the 1960s several southern cities experienced ghetto insurrections similar to those that occurred in northern cities. The Deacons for Defense and Justice was formed in Louisiana in 1965 to protect blacks and white civil rights workers from nightriders. It was one of the first black organizations formed with a mission of "defensive violence." White southerners have as much reason as their fellow whites in other regions to fear the violent aspect of Black Power.

Migration to the North

Even before the urbanization of the South was accelerated, black southerners began a great trek to the cities of the North. During the early stages of this migration white southerners opposed the movement. Sheriffs in many rural counties made life hazardous for labor recruiters who sought to lure "their" cheap black workers to Detroit and Chicago. As southern dependence on farm laborers lessened, this opposition disappeared. When the structure of segregation began to be threatened, some white southerners actually encouraged blacks to move out of the region.

This great migration had indirect but significant consequences for the South. First, it produced a black political power base in national politics, founded on the concentration of black voters in key political wards in the North. The Compromise of 1877, in which the white North tacitly left the white South to deal with "the Negro problem" in its own way, was gradually abrogated as northern white politicians became more responsive to their black constituents. The Democratic party, historically the party of the South, became also the party of the black man. Many white southern Democrats began to see themselves as an oppressed minority in an increasingly liberal party. In 1948 J. Strom Thurmond of South Carolina led a revolt against the interventionist tendencies of the national party. This revolt was to continue until it changed the whole character of southern politics, but it could not stop the growing pressure on the South to reform. Eventually, as the result of Supreme Court decisions and federal laws, black southerners were able to add their votes to the base of black political power.

The second indirect consequence of the great migration of black southerners did not become evident until much later. In the 1960s, the decade of the urban insurrections, the fact was belatedly brought home to whites of all regions that the Negro problem was a national problem. *De facto* segregation was "discovered" in the North and West. It became inescapably evident that there were large numbers of nonsouthern whites who, when confronted with the physical presence of the black American, were unwilling to share their schools, their neighborhoods, their unions, and their tax dollars with him. This brought anguish to nonsouthern whites, liberal and conservative alike, although for different reasons. It provided a perverted sort of consolation to many white southerners, however. No longer was the accusing finger pointed at the South alone; the long-standing charge that Yankees were hypocritical in their criticism of white southerners seemed to be validated. Most importantly, there appeared to be a possibility of a new unity with white Americans of other regions who could now begin to understand the ancient problem of the South. The theme of law and order became highly palatable to white southerners now that it connoted suppression of black protest rather than of white southern resistance. In 1968 some white southerners sought to create a new, national conservative alliance under the leadership of George Wallace. A larger number saw a Republican party that admitted J. Strom Thurmond to its inner councils as a feasible agency for stopping the erosion of white supremacy.

Black Militance in the South

The most obvious change in the social order of the South resulted directly from the shift of black southerners from a posture of accommodation to one of aggressive action. From the moment that Martin Luther King, Jr., led thousands of protestors into the streets of Mongomery it became evident that black southerners would no longer depend either on the good will of white southerners or on intervention from outside for changes in their status. In cities all over the South protest leaders arose to precipitate confrontations with their white fellow citizens. The old-style black leaders who had enjoyed a cordial but subservient relationship with white influentials lost both their power in the black community and the confi-

dence of their white sponsors. While indignant white southerners publicly ascribed the unrest in their communities to
"outside agitators" and "newcomers," they knew in their hearts
that there was a new spirit of rebellion even among "their
colored folks." Although the outside aid of civil rights workers,
white and black, was an essential force sustaining the civil
rights movement in the South, it should never be forgotten that
black southerners themselves participated in large numbers,
as both leaders and followers, in challenging segregation and
disenfranchisement. Enough participated to tear down the
legal structure of segregation and to cause white southerners
to view all black southerners through new eyes.

The New Racial Order

The white South fought desperately in defense of segregation. It won a partial victory by substituting tokenism for
genuine integration as the new racial order. It adopted subtle
devices, long employed in the North, for maintaining *de facto*
segregation. In some rural counties sheer terror continued to
be used to prevent black southerners from taking advantage
of their rights, but blacks became more and more difficult to
terrorize.

In most southern communities, however, the adjustment to
public desegregation following the enactment of the 1964
Civil Rights Act was amazing. The presence of black Americans in places from which they would formerly have been
barred lost its symbolic significance, particularly in the large
cities. Whether there was an internal acceptance of the new
order or not, white southerners who would once have resisted
now found it easier to ignore the "desegregated" black southerner than to challenge him. Even the minority of white
southerners who wished to establish personal, equal-status relations with individual black friends found it safer, if not
entirely comfortable, to associate with them in public.

Yet today the South is no more truly integrated than is the
rest of the nation. The black community, with its segregated
institutions, still exists. Desegregation has been a one-way

street for the most part. Blacks are admitted to certain facilities that remain predominantly white but few whites take part in "desegregation in reverse." As desegregation has become somewhat less token in nature, the same sort of "resegregation" and black protest that is occurring outside the South is appearing in the region, spurred on by the spirit of Black Power. Black students, finding themselves still a rejected or ignored minority in desegregated schools and colleges, are drawing closer to each other and challenging practices that they consider discriminatory.

During the autumn of 1968 the most dramatic illustration of the conflict between the new black southerner and the still defensive white southerner was seen in numerous protests against the playing of "Dixie" by school bands. Although it is true that ardent segregationists have made it a symbol of white resistance in recent years, the tune has had a much longer history as a regional symbol. For years both "The Star-Spangled Banner" and "Dixie" were played and equally honored at public events. This time-honored tradition was unchallenged in a segregated South.

As the number of black students in some desegregated schools increased to the point that they felt a sense of power, they began to challenge the "southern national anthem" as a symbol of slavery and an insult to their race. In one high school a group of black students attacked the band as it started to play the song during half-time at a football game. Some school administrators sought to avoid trouble by banning "Dixie." In Florida one legislator responded by introducing a bill to make it illegal for administrators to take such action (it later became law). He said:

> We're drifting away from so many of our traditions because of what people call animosities, hate inside of people. Everybody's afraid they are going to hurt somebody's feelings.
> You know there's no offense to anyone. It's a song of the South. There's tradition in it.[28]

More serious, of course, than this primarily symbolic issue have been demands by black students for black studies programs, the admission of more black students to white universities, and other concessions similar to those that have occasioned controversy in universities in other regions. Administrators of *de facto* black colleges also found themselves under fire from students infused with the spirit of Black Power.

An oft-repeated, indeed trite, prediction of hope for the betterment of race relations in the South has been that "the South would become more like the rest of the nation." There are numerous signs that the prediction is valid, but whether it constitutes a basis for optimism about the status of the black southerner becomes increasingly questionable. The strain imposed by massive black migration to northern cities has torn asunder the veil that had masked nonsouthern forms of racism. Years ago in Chicago a black migrant from Mississippi told the author, "The main difference between Chicago and the South is that here we can fight back; the white people don't like us in either place." Now the black southerner dares to fight back in his homeland. Race relations are becoming more tense, hostile, and competitive.

In this respect the South is indeed becoming more like the urban industrial North, but in all regions of the United States the potential for racial polarization and conflict is growing. The socially and physically mobile white middle class in the South may be especially vulnerable to the status insecurity engendered by the threat of Black Power and the inadequate but much-heralded efforts of the federal government to provide compensatory treatment for black Americans. In this sense a large bloc of white southerners are similar to members of white ethnic groups in the North who, having just climbed from the bottom rungs of the social ladder, feel their new status threatened by the aggressive demands of blacks and the sympathetic response such demands receive from a secure white elite. Together these threatened people may become the source of a new wave of political reaction in a nation that requires radical solutions for the problems of its minority of poor people, yet cannot persuade the affluent majority to accept such solutions. These people, who can hardly be called "new rich" but rather "recently poor," constitute a special kind of minority group, insecure, defensive, and potentially aggressive.

Notes

1 Rudolf Heberle, "The Changing Social Stratification of the South," *Social Forces*, 38 (October 1959), 43.

2 See Wilbert E. Moore and Robin M. Williams, "Stratification in the Ante-Bellum South," *American Sociological Review*, 7 (1942), 343–351.

3 William H. Nicholls, *Southern Tradition and Regional Progress* (Chapel Hill: University of North Carolina Press, 1960), p. 49.

4 W. J. Cash, *The Mind of the South* (New York: Knopf, 1941).

5 Heberle, *op. cit.*, p. 44.

6 Hortense Powdermaker, *After Freedom* (New York: Atheneum, 1968), p. 15.

7 *Ibid.*, p. 19.

8 Heberle, *op. cit.*, p. 45.

9 See William B. Hesseltine and David L. Smiley, *The South in American History* (Englewood Cliffs, N.J.: Prentice-Hall, 1960), pp. 399–411.

10 Nicholls, *op. cit.*, p. 23.

11 J. Kenneth Morland, *The Millways of Kent* (Chapel Hill: University of North Carolina Press, 1958), p. 26.

12 Nicholls, *op. cit.*, pp. 55–56.

13 Leonard Reissman, "Social Development and the Urban South," *Journal of Social Issues*, 22 (January 1966), 106.

14 See Gunnar Myrdal, *An American Dilemma* (New York: Harper and Brothers, 1944) pp. 251–270.

15 *U.S. Bureau of the Census, United States Census of Population, 1960*, vol. 1, part 1 (Washington, D.C.: Government Printing Office, 1963), table 132.

16 Leonard Reissman, "Urbanization in the South," in John C. McKinney and Edgar T. Thompson (eds.), *The South in Continuity and Change* (Durham, N.C.: Duke University Press, 1965), pp. 79–100.

17 *Ibid.*, p. 96.

[18] Charles O. Lerche, Jr., *The Uncertain South* (Chicago: Quadrangle, 1964), p. 257.

[19] Edwin M. Yoder, "W. J. Cash after a Quarter of a Century," in Willie Morris (ed.), *The South Today* (New York: Harper & Row, 1965), p. 92.

[20] Malcolm Johnson, "I Declare," Tallahassee *Democrat,* October 21, 1968, p. 1.

[21] James W. Silver, *Mississippi: The Closed Society* (New York: Harcourt, Brace & World, 1963).

[22] John Hope Franklin, "The Two Worlds of Race: A Historical View," *Daedalus,* 94 (Fall 1965), 917.

[23] See Lewis Killian and Charles Grigg, "Race Relations in an Urbanized South," *Journal of Social Issues,* 22 (January 1966), 20–22.

[24] Carl F. Grindstaff, "The Negro, Urbanization, and Relative Deprivation in the Deep South," *Social Problems,* 15 (Winter 1968), 352.

[25] Daniel C. Thompson, *The Negro Leadership Class* (Englewood Cliffs, N.J.: Prentice-Hall, 1963), p. 123.

[26] Philip M. Hauser, "Demographic Factors in the Integration of the Negro," *Daedalus,* 94 (Fall 1965), 863–864.

[27] Killian and Grigg, *op. cit.,* p. 24.

[28] "Solons Uphold 'Dixie'," Tallahassee *Democrat,* April 19, 1969, p. 3.

Chapter 4 ◉ Marginal White Southerners

While other parts of the United States have been marked by exotic diversity and multiple conflicts because of the variety of ethnic minorities they encompassed, group differences in the South have been overshadowed by the great division between white and black. A secondary line of demarcation has been drawn between southerners and Yankees. Actually the transplanted Yankees who have spent much of their lives in the South have not constituted a distinct ethnic group, even though they are not "real" southerners. Nor have the major religious minorities of the United States, Roman Catholics and Jews, been at the center of as much conflict over so long a period of time in the South as they have been in the cities of the Northeast.

The relative lack of conflict in the latter case is somewhat surprising, since the white southerner has seemed the epitome of the "WASP"—the Old American, Bible belt, white Protestant. Lillian Smith, a white southerner herself, identifies the southern white version of Protestantism as one of the major supports of southern racist traditions. In *Killers of the Dream* she contends that the liberal white southerner began to be liberated from the bonds of racism as "the lessons taught him as a Christian, a white man, an American, a puritan, began to contradict each other."[1] Not all white southerners, even those who were native born, were directly exposed to this sort of religious tradition, however. Some grew up in Catholic or Jewish homes.

Although many Catholics and Jews living in the South today are recent migrants from other regions, there have always been members of these faiths who could trace their southern ancestry back to the days of the Old South. In Savannah, Georgia, some Jewish families are descended from a small group of Spanish refugees who were given asylum by General James Oglethorpe when he established the Georgia colony. During the period of persecution of Catholics in England, some Catholic families fled to the southern colonies for refuge, and there were French and Spanish Catholics in Louisiana before the territory was purchased by the United States. The Roman Catholic dioceses of Charleston and Richmond date back to 1820. The oldest diocese in the South is that of New Orleans, established in 1793.

When the test of conformity to southern white racial orthodoxy is applied, it must be concluded that historically these marginal white southerners have been "good southerners" even though during certain periods they have been attacked as enemies of "the southern way of life." In recent years Catholics and Jews have been looked to as potential sources of liberalism on racial questions in the South, no doubt because of the unequivocal condemnation of segregation by the Roman Catholic hierarchy and the long fight against prejudice of the Anti-Defamation League of B'nai B'rith. The available historical and sociological evidence indicates, however, that regional loyalty has been as important to them as it has been to their white Protestant neighbors. In terms of attitudes toward the black American and his problems, the Jewish or Catholic liberal has been a deviant member of his group as much as has any other southern white liberal.

Catholics and the Civil War

At the time of Secession, there were eleven Catholic dioceses in the South, but there were not a great many Catholics. All of the dioceses taken together "would not have constituted one large diocese"[2] anywhere else in the country. Catholics were more numerous in the North, and their numbers there had recently been augmented by the great influx of Irish immigrants. One reaction to this wave of immigration had been the rise of the Know-Nothing party. Although it made some inroads in the South, the appeal of the Know-Nothing movement was essentially greatest in the northern states and in the South its anti-Catholic stand was a political liability.[3]

One reason that Roman Catholics were in relatively good standing in the South on the eve of the Civil War was the fact that bishops throughout the nation failed to display any strong support for the abolitionist movement. This movement included many fanatical Protestants among its leaders and some, like William Lloyd Garrison, were anti-Union. Because the United States Constitution, as interpreted by the Supreme Court, protected slavery, Garrison denounced the document as "a covenant with death and an agreement with Hell." His ire was aroused particularly by the Dred Scott decision handed down by Chief Justice Roger Taney. Coincidentally, Taney was a devout Catholic from Maryland who, although he had freed his own slaves, regarded slavery as a necessity as long as blacks remained in the United States.[4]

Roman Catholics found little to attract them in the abolition movement, for they cherished the Constitution with its guarantees of religious freedom, regarded the revolutionary spirit of the abolitionists as another manifestation of the anti-authoritarian spirit of Protestantism, and feared the prospect of war. Many of the rank and file of northern Catholics were Irish laborers who were afraid that emancipation of the slaves would be followed by a deluge of black workers who would compete with them for their jobs. During the war some of these Irish Catholics expressed their fear of free black labor in draft riots, which started with attacks on recruiting offices and ended with indiscriminate assaults on black people. Thus Catholics in the North were able to support the war as a defense of the union but had little enthusiasm for it as a struggle to free the slaves. The Catholic bishops did, for the most part, view slavery as an evil but they did not espouse immediate emancipation as a solution.

Catholics in the South found it easier to support their side of the conflict wholeheartedly. Once the Confederacy was established and accepted in the South as a legitimate government, the southern bishops found no difficulty in supporting this new civil authority. The Confederate constitution followed the Constitution of the United States in most of its provisions, including the guarantee of religious freedom.

Catholic laymen rallied to the new flag. The first commander of the Confederate Army was General Pierre G. T. Beauregard, a Catholic from Louisiana. When, early in the war, he made an appeal for church bells to be used to make ammunition the Catholic response was generous.[5] Prayers for the success of southern arms were offered in Catholic churches throughout the Confederacy. The parish in Natchez even had its own "southern holy day." In thanksgiving for the fact that the city had been only slightly damaged during a bombardment in 1862, the feast of Corpus Christi was declared a holy day of obligation and was so observed until 1913.[6]

The Roman Catholic Church in the United States was not torn by the Civil War into two branches, northern and southern, as were many of the Protestant denominations. The position of Catholics in the Confederacy has been summed up in this way:

> It is clear, then, that the bishops of the south were not unionists, but defenders of the rights of states and abettors of the confederacy. At least, they accepted it as a fact. Slavery was regarded as compatible with Christianity, and not devoid of advantages for the slaves. The elimination of abuses was recommended. The Catholic attitude toward abolitionism had ingratiated the Church to an extent with the southerners and made it possible to ascribe a goodly share of the war guilt to the Protestant clergy in states that were overwhelmingly Protestant. Although the bishops of the south differed from those of the north, their devotion to the Church did not suffer.[7]

Jews and the Confederacy

In 1860 most of the Jews in the United States lived in the North. The South had not shared proportionately in the immigration from northern and central Europe that took place between 1848 and 1860. Yet two Jews, neither of them strong religionists, had been elected to the United States Senate from southern states—Judah P. Benjamin from Louisiana, and David Yulee from Florida. There was some prejudice against Jews in the region, but (despite much criticism) Jefferson Davis appointed Benjamin attorney general when he formed the first cabinet of the Confederacy.

Whatever their status may have been in the South, Jewish southerners were loyal to the Confederacy and supported slavery with greater unity than their northern coreligionists opposed it. One historian has observed: "If the rabbis of the North were in . . . thorough disagreement about the Jewish approach to slavery and abolitionism, it is not surprising to find that their Southern colleagues gave complete support to the slave system."[8]

Like some Catholics, many northern Jews opposed abolitionism because they "viewed the War as a disaster for North and South" and "feared a seizure of power by fanatical abolitionists who would then endanger the civil and political liberties of Jews."[9] On the other hand, "With ties to the plantation economy and subject to the passions of the times, the majority of Southern Jews were for the continuation of the slavery system."[10]

When secession was followed by war, Jewish men joined the Confederate Army and prayers for a southern victory were offered in the temples. The unity of Jews with other southerners is symbolized by words from a prayer for use by Jewish soldiers composed and distributed by a Richmond rabbi:

> This once happy country is enflamed by the fury of war; a menacing enemy is arrayed against the rights, liberties and freedom of this, our Confederacy; . . . Here I stand now with many thousands of the sons of the sunny South, to face the foe, to drive him back, and to defend our natural rights, O Lord. . . . Be unto the Army of the Confederacy as thou were of old, unto us, thy chosen people—Inspire them with patriotism![11]

Jews served in many units of the Confederate Army, and two Jewish companies were recruited, one at West Point,

Georgia, and the other at Macon. The sacrifices made by individuals did not save Jews in the South from becoming scapegoats for other southerners during the course of the war, however. Just as in the North, Jews in the South were accused of profiteering and "extortion." In some southern towns resolutions were passed denouncing Jews and there were raids on Jewish stores. Judah P. Benjamin's unpopularity increased as the fortunes of the Confederacy waned, and he was repeatedly denounced as the chief source of the government's inability to win the war.

Thus the stereotype of Jews as greedy, profiteering merchants contributed to outbursts of anti-Semitism in both the North and the South. The southern variety had an especially fertile soil in which to grow:

> Additional social factors peculiar to life in the South tended to strengthen and heighten the reaction to Jews: a general dislike of all aliens and foreigners which, during the War, created the legend that the Union Army was a band of German and Irish hirelings and mercenaries, while the Confederate Army was said to be exclusively native; a wide-spread suspicion of the merchant and storekeeper, typical of a society dominated by the plantation owner and farmer; a deeper commitment than existed in the North to fundamentalist "Bible" Christianity; the intensified emotional depression as the War dragged on from year to year and Confederate chances for victory became more slight with each passing month.[12]

The loyalty of southern Jews to the Confederacy does not seem to have been diminished by this lack of appreciation. When federal troops occupied New Orleans and military authorities ordered all citizens to take the oath of allegiance to the United States or go behind the Confederate lines, the rabbi and most of the congregation refused to take the oath and were deported.[13] Judah P. Benjamin remained loyal to the bitter end and, after Lee's surrender, fled to England and never returned to the United States.

In spite of the bigotry manifested by the rise of the Ku Klux Klan during Reconstruction, neither Jews nor Catholics were targets of southern white Protestant extremism in the immediate postwar era. Blacks and Yankees bore the brunt of the defeated South's hostility. It was not until the black southerner had been "put back in his place" in the New South of the twentieth century that both anti-Semitism and anti-Catholicism became prominent features of white southern bigotry.

Jews, Catholics, and Southern Demagoguery

By 1910 the black southerner had been disenfranchised and a new brand of white southern politician had risen to prominence—the race-baiting demagogue. Such politicians based their power on appeals to the race prejudice, the economic insecurity, and the religious fundamentalism of the rural, lower-class whites. One of the most influential of this breed was the former Populist, Tom Watson of Georgia.

In 1913, partly because of Watson's influence, the white South became the setting for one of the most brutal displays of anti-Semitic hysteria and violence in the nation's history. A young Jew, Leo Frank, manager of a pencil factory in Atlanta but a native of Brooklyn, was accused of the rape and murder of Mary Phagan, a worker in the factory. "Frank's guilt or innocence of the charge of rape-murder soon became irrelevant as Tom Watson and his following turned the legal process into an anti-Semitic shambles."[14] "Little Mary Phagan" became a folk-heroine. Ironically, Frank had come to Atlanta because he was the nephew of a Confederate veteran and leader in the local Jewish community. His white southern connections did him no good, however. He was convicted on highly questionable, circumstantial evidence and, after his death sentence had been commuted to life imprisonment, was kidnapped from the prison and lynched. The clemency that had been shown by Governor John M. Slaton in commuting the sentence destroyed his own political career in Georgia.

The vicious propaganda through which Watson had openly encouraged the lynching had a quite different effect on its author's fortunes:

> For Watson, however, the Frank case was the beginning of a new career as an anti-Semite. He had discovered that attacks on the Jews greatly improved his newspaper circulation and income, which had been falling off as his readers got bored with his endless anti-Catholic tirades. And his political stock rose: in 1920 he was elected to the seat he had held thirty years before in the United States Senate . . .[15]

The loss of popular interest in Watson's anti-Catholicism did not signify that Catholics were no longer vulnerable as political targets in this ultra-white, super-Protestant New South. Soon after the end of World War I a new Ku Klux Klan arose, a Klan that spread outside the region and became a force in national politics. This new Klan added Jews and Catholics to the black man on their list of enemies. Anti-Semitism and anti-Catholicism gave the Invisible Empire an appeal to small-town Protestants outside the South, in regions where these varieties of bigotry had a longer history. At the same time:

> In the South especially, anti-Semitism and anti-Catholicism were usually linked in Klan propaganda. Tammany Hall was denounced as the machine through which undesirable aliens planned first to seize control of the Democratic party, then of the government in Washington. . . . The flames of religious bigotry were fed by charges that the Catholic church had organized southern Negroes without regard to regional mores.[16]

The high-water mark of southern anti-Catholicism was reached in the presidential campaign of 1928. Alfred E. Smith, the first Catholic to run for president, proved to be also the first Democratic candidate who failed to carry the "Solid South." One of the major factors contributing to this failure was the appeal to anti-Catholicism spread through both a whispering campaign and an overt attack by some Protestant clergymen, such as Methodist Bishop James Cannon. Many poorly educated white southerners believed the stories that Roman Catholic churches contained stores of arms for a revolution and that the Pope would dictate policy to a Catholic president.

Anti-Catholicism was not so significant thirty-two years later when another Catholic, John F. Kennedy, ran for president. While some anti-Catholic propaganda was distributed surreptitiously by prosegregration organizations, the insurgent black American had once again become the focus of prejudice. Kennedy's failure to carry the southern states of Tennessee, Virginia, and Florida must be ascribed to factors other than religious prejudice. The victory of Dwight D. Eisenhower in 1952 had marked the permanent end of the Democratic unity of the South and the beginning of a "Republican revolution," which was "a product of the social forces unleashed by the urbanization of the South and the struggle of the Southern Negro for political and civil rights."[17]

Despite these historic evidences of the capacity of southern white Protestants to turn on Jews and Catholics as aliens and enemies, southern anti-Semitism and anti-Catholicism have differed from the types found in northern cities. Except in the case of some atypical Florida resort cities, such as Miami Beach, and in the special case of Louisiana, Jews and Catholics have been abstract, symbolic objects of prejudice rather than highly visible groups. When, in 1862, a grand jury in Talbot County, Georgia, condemned the "evil and unpatriotic conduct" of Jewish merchants, there was only one Jewish family in the county. When this Jewish merchant expressed his grief at this condemnation, numerous citizens of the community, including every member of the grand jury, "assured him that there had been no intention to reflect upon *his* business ethics or *his* faith!"[18] As for the Catholics, Edmund A. Moore said of the people who responded to Ku Klux Klan propaganda in the 1920s:

> The strongholds of the Ku Klux Klan were the small towns and villages, where the older American stock dominated. The great majority of citizens in these com-

munities were Protestants who knew very little of Catholics or of the immigrant stock of distant cities, but this in no way lessened their sense of apprehensiveness.[19]

The Assimilation of Catholics and Jews in the South

In many of these small towns and villages the very small minority of Jewish and Catholic families were well integrated into the life of the total community. They were not segregated, voluntarily or involuntarily, into ethnic enclaves. Successful businessmen and their families were accepted in civic and even social clubs in many small towns. Their children dated Protestant boys or girls, although, especially in the case of Jews, they were not likely to marry them. These same children had no difficulty in gaining admittance to universities in the South. In fact, Jewish students often found their numbers augmented by northern Jewish refugees who had been kept out of universities in their own states by the quota system. Jewish sororities and fraternities did flourish, for the Greek system was "Christian" in an invidious sense. Catholic students encountered no such exclusion.

Certainly Jews and Catholics have never been totally assimilated in the white, Protestant South but, then, many of them have not sought loss of their religious identity. Except during certain episodes of anti-Semitism or anti-Catholicism, they have found this identity less of a barrier to economic, political, and social equality than they would have in other regions where larger Jewish and Catholic minorities existed. In turn, other white southerners have served as a powerful reference group for them according to modern sociological studies.

In his study of a southern parish in the late 1940s, Joseph Fichter found no Catholic vote as such and no distinctive Catholic political philosophy. Moreover, very few white Catholics in the city he studied "seemed to have any ethical qualms over the racist aspect of the Dixiecrat program" in the 1948 presidential election.[20] In direct questions concerning racial segregation Fichter found that the great majority of his subjects were opposed to integration of either parochial schools or the parish itself (a separate black parish existed). In summary, he said of these southern Catholics, "In their social and political attitudes they tend toward the traditional and conservative ideas prevalent in Riverside."[21]

Over ten years later William T. Liu analyzed Roman Catholics in a small southern city as a marginal group.[22] Most of these Catholics had migrated to the South during or after World War II. The study was conducted at a time when the Church's condemnation of racial segregation was in sharp and open conflict with white southern mores. The powerful influence of the southern ethos was reflected in the fact that strength of identification with the Catholic Church did not prove to be related to attitudes on the issues of race and the rights of labor, areas in which the white southern community tended to be more conservative than Catholic doctrine. The stronger the identification with the South, the more southern were attitudes on race and labor, no matter how devout a Catholic subject might be in other respects. Moreover, the longer the Catholic had lived in the community, the more likely he was to disagree with the official doctrine of the Church on racial segregation.

One of the most significant of Liu's findings supports the suggestion that being a Catholic hardly constitutes a barrier to assimilation into the life of the white southern community. The subjects who were highest in what he called "catholicity" tended also to be highest in social participation in the secular activities of the community. In other words, the Catholic parish and its life did not represent a subcommunity competing with the larger community for the time and loyalty of its members. Indeed, Liu suggested that "like members of the Protestant denominations, some Catholics in the South participated in the functions of the parish for the sake of general social conformity."[23]

The hierarchy of the Roman Catholic Church, including the archbishops of several southern dioceses, has been vigorous in denouncing segregation as unchristian as well as unlawful. Catholic schools and colleges, like Spring Hill College in Mobile and several parochial schools in North Carolina, were among the first schools in the South to be desegregated. The problem that ecclesiastical authority faces when it encounters white southern orthodoxy was dramatized by the conflict between clergy and laity in New Orleans, the most Catholic state in the region. There Archbishop Rummel was faced by a revolt of organized Catholic laymen when he announced his intention of desegregating both parochial schools and parishes. The controversy was carried all the way to the Vatican before the laymen were convinced that they could not fight the archbishop successfully.

No systematic studies of the attitudes of Jews in the South are available for comparison with the findings of Fichter and Liu. Some prosegregation propaganda has stressed the strong support rendered the NAACP by Jewish philanthropists, suggesting that all Jews must be integrationists. Harry Golden, author and for many years editor and publisher of the *Carolina Israelite*, has been one of the white South's most effective critics of segregation, largely because of his humorous approach. His writings and speeches have reinforced the stereotype of the liberal Jew. Not so well known are Rabbi Benjamin Schultz, of Mississippi, and Charles Bloch, a prominent lawyer in Macon, Georgia. Rabbi Schultz openly supported the White Citizens Council in Mississippi, even though he was a recent immigrant from New York.[24] Bloch was one of the leaders of the Dixiecrat revolt at the Democratic national convention in Philadelphia in 1948.

In *The South Strikes Back*, Hodding Carter, III, gives his interpretation of why the White Citizens Council consistently played down anti-Semitism in its appeals:

> One reason the Councils do not move against the Jewish citizens of Mississippi is that in many cases they do, in truth, share the Councils' views. Another is that while a latent anti-Semitism may exist in the white Christian community, it is not strong enough to make its positive expression worth while unless there should be some indication that the Jewish members of the community were going to question Southern racial attitudes. Few Southern Jews have openly done so. Accordingly, they are ac-

cepted as conforming members of the white community
and not subjects for outright Council discipline.[25]

It might be said that there has been *enough* latent anti-
Semitism in the South to make good southerners out of many
Jews. Their marginality has placed a high premium on conformity to the regional mores. As it has been said of black
Americans' resistance to communism, "It's bad enough to be
black in America without being red, too!" it might be said,
"It's risky enough to be a Jew in the South without being a
'nigger-lover' too!" If discrimination against Jews in the South
were harsher and more consistent, more southern Jews might
see black southerners as partners in a common struggle against
racism. Staff members of the Anti-Defamation League working in the South have reported, however, that they have had
difficulty in persuading loyal members of the organization to
make common cause with black men at the risk of their
precarious but comfortable status in the predominantly WASP
community.

The evidence indicates that Jews have encountered higher
barriers to assimilation as white southerners than have Catholics, particularly in the larger cities in which one could speak
realistically of a "Jewish community." In 1950, the 9,100 Jews
in New Orleans constituted 1.9 percent of the total white population; the 10,217 Jews in Atlanta were 4.8 percent.[26] A study
done in New Orleans and a similar one in Jacksonville showed
that no more than 10 percent of marriages of Jews in these
cities were mixed marriages.[27] As has been suggested previously, it seems that no matter how well accepted they may
be in southern communities Jews still tend to marry within
their own small religious group.

In New Orleans and Atlanta, employed Jews were found to
be heavily concentrated in trade, both wholesale and retail,
and in the professions. They were not found to be employed
in manufacturing, particularly at the lower skill levels, to the
same extent as other white southerners. The urban Jew in the
South is much more likely to be upper or upper middle class
than is the non-Jewish white southerner.[28]

Solomon Sutker's study of the Jewish community of Atlanta in the 1940s showed that in this city there was indeed a Jewish community with a social life of its own. There were three Jewish social clubs in the city, although these owed their existence primarily to the fact that Jews were excluded from the other major social clubs. (A study by Ben Kaplan of three small towns in Louisiana showed that the relatively few Jewish families in such towns did not encounter similar exclusion.)[29] Sutker characterized the marginality of Atlanta Jews in these words:

> Actually there is some social intermingling between Jew and non-Jew but it is not on a common club-membership basis. Social intercourse with non-Jews is most frequent with Jews who are wealthy and whose families have been resident in Atlanta for several generations. It also takes place between Jews and non-Jews who hold liberal points of view on social, economic and political issues. However, on the social level that constitutes "top society" the position of the Jew is very insecure—his status is that of an occasional guest but never that of the completely accepted member.[30]

Atlanta also supports a number of other Jewish organizations that would not be found in smaller southern communities; for example, the Jewish Community Council, the Children's Service Agency, the Federation for Jewish Social Service, the Labor Zionists, and both a chapter and the regional office of the Anti-Defamation League. These organizations provide the basis for the existence of an "organizational elite" of Jewish professional workers. These professionals constitute an influence that may help to maintain the separateness of the Jewish community in Atlanta, for Sutker remarked:

> The various members of the organizational elite were born and/or reared either in the northern cities of the United States or Europe in practically every instance. . . . Apparently there are very few persons in the South, even in proportion to its total Jewish population, that train either for the rabbinate or for any professional secular positions in Jewish communal life. Most of the

organizational elite appear to have deeper roots in a more pervasive Jewish cultural background than ordinarily is to be found among the general Jewish population of Atlanta.[31]

As the South becomes more urbanized and more outsiders, including Jews, migrate to the region, Jews may come to constitute a more pluralistic ethnic group than they have in the past. There may be larger Jewish communities in more southern cities as the South, in this respect, becomes more like the North. Southern Jews may become less southern than their history shows them to have been in the past. In addition, an increase in Catholics may lead to growth of larger parishes; however, Liu's findings suggest this will not lead to the development of Catholic communities in which members may find a separate social world.

Transplanted Yankees

Next to the black man, the Yankee has been historically one of the chief targets of white southern prejudice. He has been equated with a long succession of "meddlers": abolitionists, marauding blue-coats, Carpetbaggers, communist (meaning "labor union") agitators, civil rights workers, and, most recently, Washington bureaucrats. In other roles, however, Yankees—and their money—have been welcome. At least since the beginning of World War II much of the growth and the increasing prosperity of the South has been accompanied and sustained by the migration of white people from other regions as permanent residents. Many of them have moved to the South in the capacity of managers or skilled workers in new branches of northern-owned industries or businesses. There has been a resulting "growth of a Yankee population of middle-class, white-collar and *elite* manual workers in the South."[32] (See Appendix, Table 6, for whites born in other divisions living in South in 1960.)

Some of the migrants have been teachers or college professors. In some areas many of the newcomers have been retired workers. Rather than being aggressive, meddling invaders, these Yankees have been virtually invited to move to the South as a land of opportunity and pleasant living. Many have been lured by the blandishments of chambers of commerce or tourist bureaus. Even southern universities have tried to improve their national images by recruiting faculty and graduate students from outside the region, implicitly admitting to a conception that brands higher education in the South as provincial and inferior.

Like other marginal white southerners, the transplanted Yankee gains greatest acceptance if he is sensitive to, and considerate of, the slowly changing racial attitudes of the natives. He may be excused for an initial affront to local customs on the grounds that he "doesn't understand the situation down here." If he appears to be a crusader, however, he arouses the dormant hostility of conservative white southerners. Often the liberal in matters of race relations is equated with the Yankee. The author, disliked as a white liberal by some segments of the population in the northern Florida city where he taught, often received suggestions that "he go back where he came from," advanced by people who knew him only by reputation. These people were unaware that he had "come South" to Florida after a childhood in the neighboring state of Georgia.

Optimistic liberals often look on these migrants from the North as a possible leavening influence on southern racial attitudes. It seems reasonable to believe that people not raised in the racial order of the South would indeed introduce an element of heterodoxy that would speed up the pace of social change. There is little evidence that they have, however, and there are many logical arguments as to why they should not be expected to.

To the extent that migration to the South is connected with employment, the question must be raised: "Why do businesses and industries relocate?" The most unlikely reason is that they desire to reform the natives of the host community. Ministers and college professors (and civil rights activists) may sometimes move to the South as missionaries, but businessmen and manufacturers do not. Their motives are economic. These motives have included new markets, tax abatements, sources of raw materials, and avoidance of union-management conflicts. One of the things the Yankee manager of a southern plant least wants is to get into a fight with the local population over race relations. The sociologist Herbert Blumer, in arguing that industrialization does not necessarily lead to greater racial democracy, says:

> The manager of an industrial plant who may be willing to hire workers of a subordinate racial group for high-level jobs or promote them to advanced positions suited to their aptitudes or skills may definitely refrain from doing so in order not to provoke difficulties with other workers. This is a *rational* decision which has occurred innumerable times in industrial establishments introduced into a society with a strongly established racial system.[33]

Observers of the effects of industrialization on the status of the black southerner have reached a similar conclusion. Munro S. Edmundson and David R. Norsworthy comment:

> It is clear that the industrialisation of the Negro in the South has a long way to go. The principal movement to date has been from the bottom of a rural status system to the bottom of an urban one. Nearly half of the experienced Negro women workers in the South in 1960 were still domestic servants. It has been argued that industrialisation will bring the Negro into new jobs and consequently new relations with whites destructive of the old stereotypes of master and slave. Perhaps it will, but it has not done so yet.

They go on to say:

> Representatives of industry in the South, even those born in the North and speaking for large national corporations, may go so far as to adopt the Federally sponsored "equal opportunity" policy and genuinely try to make it work, but they made it plain that "we are not crusaders."[34]

One of the tasks of the Yankee manager is to maintain good community relations. To do so, he does not become a member of the NAACP or join a march protesting racial discrimination. He joins the chamber of commerce, affiliates with the church of his choice, and seeks membership in Rotary, Kiwanis, or some other civic club. In doing so, he exposes himself to the conservative end of the spectrum of white southern opinion, and he is not likely to challenge rudely the pronouncements of his new associates on "the way we handle the race problem down here."

Nor does the retiree move to the South as a crusader. Often he comes from a northern city in which the expanding black ghetto was a source of vague or even immediate concern to him. Peace and relaxation, not controversy and racial strife, are what he seeks. In Rome he not only does as the Romans do; he may even come to admire their customs.

A special class of transplanted Yankee includes the military servicemen who are assigned for tours of duty in the South. During World War I and continuously since World War II the combination of the mild climate, the availability of land, and the seniority of southern congressmen has led to a concentration of military and naval installations in the region. The adoption of a policy of across-the-board integration during the Truman administration made the armed forces a potentially subversive presence in the South. The enthusiasm of white southern congressmen and chambers of commerce for having military installations near their communities did not diminish, however, for integration typically stopped at the gates of the posts. In 1952 at one air base in Georgia, black airmen complained that drivers of city busses stopped at the gate on leaving the base and ordered black passengers to move to the rear of the bus. Although service clubs, swimming pools, and other recreational facilities on the post were integrated, black servicemen going on pass were still restricted to the amenities offered by the black sections of nearby towns. Occasionally the influence of the community even reached into the base. Service clubs that were supposed to be integrated often became resegregated for the simple reason that black servicemen felt that they had nowhere else to go, while whites had a wider range of choices. The public accommodation section of the Civil Rights Act of 1964 brought about some changes, but it had no effect on the problem of the limited availability of off-base housing for the families of black servicemen. The armed services still find southern customs highly resistant to their influence. In 1969 one of the chief complaints of black marines who engaged in violent protest at Camp Lejeune, North Carolina, was that they still encountered segregation and discrimination in towns near the base. Servicemen, white or black, who attempt to challenge local customs even when they are off duty are likely to find themselves embroiled with the civilian police and courts. They run the additional risk of becoming suspect as troublemakers within their military organization; the military police and commanding officers cannot simply ignore the charges of their civilian counterparts. At the trial of Captain Howard Levy at Ft. Bragg, North Carolina, the defense alleged that his involvement in civil rights activities in nearby Fayetteville had contributed to his growing disfavor in the eyes of his superior officers.

The assumption that transplanted Yankees constitute a liberalizing influence in the white South also rests on a questionable generalization concerning differences in white attitudes, rather than practices, between regions. Many attitude studies (too many of them based on samples of college students) do suggest real regional differences in response to abstract questions about black Americans. Whites growing up outside the South may have been accustomed to desegregated public facilities, transportation, and, to some extent, work places. Some, however, have lived in communities where there were no blacks. Urban dwellers may have been isolated from contact with poor black people because black poverty in the North is frequently hidden in the ghetto. In the southern community they get their first close-up view of poor, undereducated black people, particularly if they hire domestic servants. Their abstract notions of how black Americans should be treated quickly give way to approval of the traditional manner in which white southerners have dealt with the very visible proportion of black southerners among them. They may experience a personal "white backlash" in the South, just as they might have had they remained in a northern city torn by increasing racial conflict.

Finally, the white southerner of Yankee origin is, like the Jew, conscious of his marginality. The readiness with which the conservative, native-born white southerner will ask, "Where were you born?" to end an argument reminds the Yankee of this marginality. In one of his last columns the late Ralph McGill found bitter humor in the lingering prejudice against Yankees. He recounted:

> On one and the same day the United States Senate and the Atlanta Bird Club engaged in debate. In the Senate, Southern members Stennis, Long and Russell lashed out at the Northern members who were voting down a House amendment that would have enabled local school districts to perpetuate outrageously discriminating schemes and practices. Once again it was the wicked old Northern influences loosed against the South.
>
> The Atlanta Bird Club held a fervent debate on whether to join with the National Audubon Society. One gentle Southern lady, speaking in opposition, was quoted by reporters who covered the meeting as charging that the Atlanta Club had been "infiltrated with Yankees who were eager to sell out to the Audubon Society."
>
> "You can't tell me our Yankee members are not behind this," she said.

McGill concluded:

> "The War" has been over since 1865 and that the old North-South prejudices should continue to be articulated with heat and rancor inescapably is a revealing commentary on the enduring qualities of such practices— a commentary both hilarious and melancholy.[35]

As the South moves under the pressure of federal law and the black revolution, some transplanted Yankees may find it easier to move with it than do most native white southerners. Some Jews and Catholics may find it easier to reconcile new patterns of race relations with those of other members of their religious groups and may therefore welcome the change. It is unlikely, however, that marginal white southerners will move much faster than the natives. The Jew or Catholic who becomes too liberal reminds his white Protestant neighbors of his religious deviance. A northern-born white who persists in challenging orthodox southern beliefs is held to be unqualified to comment intelligently on "the South's problem"; he doesn't understand it. Sooner or later he will be told that he should go back North where he belongs, for the Yankee who is a nonconformist quickly becomes a "damyankee."

Notes

1 Lillian Smith, *Killers of the Dream* (New York: Norton, 1949), p. 109.

2 Benjamin J. Blied, *Catholics and the Civil War* (Milwaukee: St. Francis Seminary, 1945), p. 53.

3 See William B. Hesseltine and David L. Smiley, *The South in American History* (Englewood Cliffs, N.J.: Prentice-Hall, 1960), pp. 242–245.

4 Blied, *op. cit.*, pp. 16–17.

5 *Ibid.*, p. 55.

6 *Ibid.*, p. 56.

7 *Ibid.*, p. 69.

8 Bertram W. Korn, *American Jewry and the Civil War* (Philadelphia: The Jewish Publication Society of America, 1951), p. 29.

9 Eugene I. Bender, "Reflections on Negro-Jewish Relationships: the Historical Dimension," *Phylon*, 30 (Spring 1969), 62.

10 *Ibid.*, p. 60.

11 Korn, *op. cit.*, p. 89.

12 *Ibid.*, p. 168.

13 *Ibid.*, pp. 47–48.

14 John P. Roche, *The Quest for the Dream* (New York: Macmillan, 1963), p. 87.

15 *Ibid.*, p. 91.

16 Edmund A. Moore, *A Catholic Runs for President* (New York: Ronald Press, 1956), p. 27.

17 John C. Topping, Jr., John R. Lazarek, and William H. Linder, *Southern Republicanism and the New South* (Cambridge, Mass.: 1966), p. 2.

[18] Korn, *op. cit.*, p. 183.

[19] Moore, *op. cit.*, p. 27.

[20] Joseph H. Fichter, *Southern Parish: Dynamics of a City Church* (Chicago: University of Chicago Press, 1951), p. 31.

[21] *Ibid.*, p. 265.

[22] William T. Liu, "The Marginal Catholics in the South: A Revision of Concepts," *American Journal of Sociology*, 65 (January 1960), 383–390.

[23] *Ibid.*, p. 388.

[24] James W. Silver, *Mississippi: The Closed Society* (New York: Harcourt, Brace & World, 1966), p. 131.

[25] Hodding Carter, III, *The South Strikes Back* (Garden City, N.J.: Doubleday, 1959), p. 172.

[26] Ben B. Seligman, "Some Aspects of Jewish Demography," in Marshall Sklare (ed.), *The Jews: Social Patterns of an American Group* (New York: Free Press, 1958), p. 51.

[27] *Ibid.*, p. 63.

[28] *Ibid.*, pp. 69–82.

[29] Ben Kaplan, *The Eternal Stranger* (New York: Bookman Associates, 1957).

[30] Solomon Sutker, "The Role of Social Clubs in the Atlanta Jewish Community," in Sklare, *op. cit.*, p. 263.

[31] Solomon Sutker, "The Jewish Organizational Elite of Atlanta, Georgia," in Sklare, *op. cit.*, p. 254.

[32] Munro S. Edmondson and David R. Norsworthy, "Industry and Race in the Southern United States," in Guy Hunter (ed.) *Industrialisation and Race Relations* (New York: Oxford University Press, 1965), p. 48.

[33] Herbert Blumer, "Industrialisation and Race Relations," in Hunter, *op. cit.*, p. 232.

[34] Edmondson and Norsworthy, *op. cit.*, p. 52.

[35] Syndicated column in the Hartford *Courant*, October 21, 1968, p. 16.

Chapter 5 ◉ White Southern Migrants

"Chicago's Hillbilly Ghetto"—so read the title of an article in *The Reporter* in 1964. The term "ghetto," first applied to Jewish enclaves, later to black slums, was here adopted to characterize a concentration of white southern people in a northern city. The author of the article described the "hill-billies" as a group that had "landed at the bottom of the pecking order," "undernourished, uneducated, unwanted, and unable to cope with a society that does not understand them or their ways."[1]

Up until this point, we have treated white southerners in their homeland, the southern region, as being analogous to a European-type minority. In Europe the term "minority" has usually referred to a group that has lived historically in a particular region and has been "forced into a strong in-solidarity by a shifting of political boundaries."[2] In the United States the concept has more often been applied to immigrant groups forced, as newcomers, to find their places in a dominant, host society. There is evidence that some, if not all, white southerners undergo the experience of the American-type minority when they migrate to other regions of their own nation. And in the twentieth century, large numbers of white southerners have sought their fortunes outside the southern homeland. (See Appendix, Table 7, for whites born in South and living in other divisions.)

The Exodus of White Southerners

One of the great fears of white southerners has been that migrants to their region would prove to be an exploitative or subversive element. Careful analysts, like Howard W. Odum, have recognized a source of greater concern—the possibility that the South would lose human wealth through selective migration. If it were clear that the people who choose to migrate from a community are those least likely to succeed, then citizens concerned with civic welfare might well say, "Good riddance!" Available evidence indicates, however, that it is not the dregs of a society that are most likely to move. This has been found to be true of white southerners.

The migration occasioned by the early years of the Great Depression stimulated extensive research on the characteristics of internal migrants.[3] A common conclusion of these studies was that migrants tend to be young adults, the age group characterized by the greatest economic productivity, and that they also tend to be persons with somewhat better than average educational ability. In a later study utilizing data from the 1940, 1950, and 1960 censuses, Henry S. Shryock, Jr., and Charles B. Nam reached a similar conclusion.[4] They found that migration out of the South was selective; migrants tended to be the middle and highly educated residents of the region. Because a similar sort of selectivity operated among migrants to the South, however, the net effect of migration was to increase the educational level of the region. Still, the South was exporting some of its better-educated sons and daughters while retaining a higher proportion of the poorly educated.

Another study shows that when hard times hit the South or any part of it, it is the more capable natives who leave. In the affluent United States of recent decades the southern Appalachian region is one of the great pockets of poverty. During the ten years between 1950 and 1960 this area lost almost a fifth of its total population through migration. Two sociologists, James S. Brown and George A. Hillery, Jr., answer the question, "Who are the migrants?" in these words: "Single persons and young families, most of whom were better educated than those they left behind and not as well educated as those they settled among."[5]

In this area of the South the net effect of migration lowered the educational level, for the reason pointed out by Brown and Hillery:

> Out-migrants and in-migrants are better educated than the Southern Appalachian population as a whole, but since out-migration has exceeded in-migration for many years, the net result has been to retard the rise in the educational level of the Region's population.[6]

This finding reinforces Shryock and Nam's cautionary statement concerning the net improvement in the educational level of the entire southern region:

> In interpreting the net improvement in the South's educational status that resulted from interregional migration, we need to recognize the considerable heterogeneity of what is often regarded as the Nation's problem region. Certain flourishing subareas (e.g., the Washington metropolitan area, metropolitan areas around the Gulf of Mexico, the Florida Gold Coast, and areas dominated by military and aerospace activities) have had relatively heavy in-migration of well-educated workers and retired persons from other regions.[7]

Howard Odum was particularly concerned about the loss of potential "stars" from the southern population. During his years as head of the sociology department at the University of North Carolina he spent many hours urging young southern sociologists to dedicate themselves to careers in the homeland, although he advised them to obtain part of their graduate education outside the South. In 1936, in *Southern Regions of the United States*, he repeated the warning of another sociologist who was a native son, T. J. Woofter, Jr.:

> Migration further exerts a selective drag on the talent of the region. This is difficult to measure at the bottom of the scale, but its effect at the top is marked. Wilson Gee has shown a 45 per cent drag of social scientists and 60 per cent of natural scientists. That is to say, 45 per

cent of the eminent social scientists who were born in the South were living outside the South and 60 per cent of the natural scientists.[8]

The South: An Intellectual Desert?

This "talent drag" no doubt results in part from an unflattering stereotype of the South as a culturally backward region. No other part of the United States has been so viciously denounced as the South was by H. L. Mencken in 1920 in his famous essay, "The Sahara of the Bozart."[9] Mencken praised the civilization of the Old South as the best the United States had ever produced. His view of the New South was quite different from that of southern boosters. He wrote:

> And yet, for all its size and all its wealth and all the "progress" it babbles of, it is almost as sterile, artistically, intellectually, culturally, as the Sahara Desert. There are single acres in Europe that house more first-rate men than all the states south of the Potomac; there are probably single square miles in America. If the whole of the late Confederacy were to be engulfed by a tidal wave tomorrow, the effect upon the civilized minority of men in the world would be but little greater than that of a flood on the Yang-tse-kiang. It would be impossible in all history to match so complete a drying-up of a civilization.[10]

Mencken perceived the South as a region governed by poor whites who he believed to be of a biologically inferior stock. Religion was characterized by "Baptist and Methodist barbarism" and education had sunk "to the Baptist seminary level." He argued that lynching was a popular "sport" because "the backward culture of the region denied the populace more seemly recreations."[11]

Despite whatever progress might have been made since Mencken's diatribe, something of the same unfavorable image of the South still survived forty years later. In 1961 Russell W. Middleton studied problems of recruitment of academic staff in the largest universities in ten southern states (Alabama, Arkansas, Florida, Georgia, Louisiana, Mississippi,

North Carolina, South Carolina, Tennessee, and Virginia).[12] He queried department chairmen in the liberal arts colleges and he also sent questionnaires to doctoral candidates at leading universities all over the United States. Fifty-two percent of the southern department chairmen believed that racial problems in the South caused them to have difficulty in recruiting competent faculty members. Among doctoral candidates the South ranked fifth out of five regions (Northeast, Far West, Middle West, Southwest, South) as a place in which these prospective faculty members would want to teach. Regardless of the state in which a southern university was located, the majority of the doctoral candidates said they would consider a position there only if the rank or salary were higher than what they were offered in other regions. This reaction was not simply a result of Yankee prejudice. Middleton analyzed the responses of native white southerners separately and concluded:

> Still, a majority even of the native southerners are reluctant to teach in most of the southern states. Surprisingly, the candidates at the southern university tend to be even more hostile to the Deep South than are the candidates at the nonsouthern universities.[13]

The image of the South as an unfavorable intellectual milieu held by these doctoral candidates is reflected in some of the reasons given for their reluctance to teach there. All of the following were listed as important disadvantages by more than half of the doctoral candidates at nonsouthern universities:[14]

Racial prejudice (73.9 percent)
Public schools may be closed over desegregation issue (66.1)
Public schools of poor quality (63.8)
Undesirable community influence on child's character and ideals (62.2)
Race problem may lead to civic unrest, violence (55.2)
Low academic standards (53.6)
Lack of academic freedom (52.7)
Police and courts do not administer justice fairly (52.5)

Thus not only the climate of racial intolerence and tension but also the aura of intellectual inferiority make the South an unattractive setting for budding intellectuals, almost as much for native sons as for other Americans. While the loss of such talent cannot be precisely measured, one refugee saw evidence that it is substantial. Willie Morris, a native of Mississippi who became editor of *Harper's*, wrote of his encounter with a fellow white southerner in New York:

> He was a "liberated Mississippian" who had just joined New York's burgeoning and implacable Southern expatriate community; he was the first of many Mississippi "exiles" I would see in the Big Cave—for, in truth, as I would come to understand, Mississippi may have been the only state in the Union (or certainly one of a half dozen in the South) which had produced a genuine set of exiles, almost in the European sense: alienated from home yet forever drawn back to it, seeking some form of personal liberty elsewhere yet obsessed with the texture and the complexity of the place from which they had departed as few Americans from other states could ever be.[15]

As internal migrants in a reunited nation, white southerners leave a homeland marked by a regional consciousness. Although they are Americans, they have another identity as southerners. It is hard for them to forget this identity and it is remarkably easy for Americans in other regions to recognize them as southerners.

The Visibility of White Southerners

In most respects white southerners are physically and culturally indistinguishable from other white Americans. Even the country "hick" from the South is almost certain to wear ready-made clothes designed and manufactured in the garment district of New York City. The white southerner speaks the same language as other Americans, but with a crucial difference—the southern accent. Although there are many southern accents and although other local accents resemble the drawl of the southerner, there is a great deal of truth to the saying, "You can recognize a southerner as soon as he opens his mouth." The white southern migrant or tourist soon becomes accustomed to being asked by waitresses or sales clerks, "What part of the South are *you* from?"

This mark of identification cuts across class lines. In Chicago in the late 1940s remarks like these were made about working-class white southern migrants:

> (An employer) I told the guard at the plant gate to tell the hillbillies that there were no openings. It was easy enough, you know. The guard could tell which ones were from the South by their speech.

> (A bartender) I shake all over everytime a cop or somebody that says you-all walks in the door.

Willie Morris, a college graduate and a successful newspaper editor, found that he was visible as a white southerner in New York because of his accent. He describes the following encounter in a crowded, swaying subway car:

> Instinctively I grabbed for something, and it turned out to be the arm of a Negro next to me; he was about my age. When the train steadied again, reverting to my old Mississippi accent as I always do under stress, I told him I was sorry. He gave me a cold stare, and then he sneered.

> "I'm sorry," I said, "I didn't have anything to hold on to. This is a hell of a way to live."

> "It beats them hills, don't it?" the man said in a strong Negro southern accent.

> "What hills?" I asked.

> "Them hills you come from with that cracker accent."[16]

In the case of the well-educated and affluent migrant, visibility as a white southerner may occasion only temporary annoyance at being stereotyped. For the less well-educated, economically marginal newcomer to a northern city, the matter is of graver consequence. He becomes a "hillbilly"[17] in the eyes of the nonsouthern dominant group, and to many of his fellow Americans the hillbilly represents a problem.

The Hillbilly Problem in the North

In 1951 Wayne University, with the assistance of the University of Michigan Survey Research Center, studied the views of Detroit residents about their city. Among the questions was one that asked members of the sample to identify "undesirable people" who were "not good to have in the city." The types of people so identified, by the percentage of subjects who named them, were:[18]

Criminals, gangsters	26 percent
Poor southern whites, hillbillies	21 percent
Transients, drifters, non-self-supporting	18 percent
Negroes	13 percent
Foreigners	6 percent

Here was evidence that at least a certain class of white southerners was conceptualized as an identifiable group, one disliked even more than Negroes, whose minority status is beyond question. The social science survey reflected a Detroit attitude that had been expressed during World War II in a hostile joke: "There are now only forty-five states in the U.S. —Tennessee and Kentucky moved to Michigan and Michigan went to hell!"

Social scientists had taken note of the presence of the white southerners as the expansion of defense industries in Detroit attracted new workers to the automobile capital. In 1935 Louis Adamic wrote in *The Nation:*

> For months now the companies have been sending their labor agents to recruit hill-billies from Kentucky, Tennessee, Louisiana and Alabama. These hill-billies are for the most part impoverished whites, "white trash" or a little better, from the rural regions.[19]

In 1941 Henry Hill Collins, in *America's Own Refugees,* commented on the already existing practice of northern industrialists who used whites from the upper South as a labor reserve:

> The great automobile factories, for instance, draw upon the labor reserves of rural Kentucky and Tennessee for their peak season requirements. During their periodic shutdowns the layed-off and unemployed in thousands return to the foothills and mountain hamlets of the Bluegrass and Volunteer States.[20]

In analyzing the causes of the Detroit race riot of 1943, Alfred M. Lee and Norman D. Humphrey identified recent white southern migrants as one of the primary contributing factors. They declared:

> The effort to make Detroit conform to Kentucky "hill-billy" and Georgia "red neck" notions of white domination is reflected in frequent white comments in busses and streetcars and bars, such as: "It wouldn't have happened down home. We know how to keep niggers in their place." "Southern niggers aren't like these bold brassy Northern niggers."[21]

Journalists have periodically discovered or rediscovered a hillbilly "minority" in other northern cities. In 1956 James Maxwell wrote an article for *The Reporter,* entitled "Down from the Hills and into the Slums." He illustrated the perception of the hillbillies held by other residents of one city, Indianapolis, with this quotation from a "native":

> Those people are creating a terrible problem in our city. They can't or won't hold a job, they flout the law constantly and neglect their children, they drink too much and their moral standards would shame an alley cat. For some reason or other, they absolutely refuse to accommodate themselves to any kind of decent, civilized life.[22]

Maxwell accepted as valid a belief held by some northern observers, that white southern "mountaineers" have a visibility that is both cultural and racial. He wrote:

In most Midwestern cities, these neighborhoods of Southern mountaineers are as easily recognizable as those made up of Italians or Jews or Negroes. The people from the mountains usually are tall, loose-limbed, and angular, with the blond hair and ruddiness traditionally associated with the English race. On the whole, both men and women are shabbily dressed—the men in sloppy, ill-fitting suits and colored shirts with garish ties, while the women seem to prefer nondescript dresses hanging loose from the shoulders. The hill folk speak with a twang of their own that sounds somewhat rustic and archaic and frequently use terms that were familiar at the time of the first Queen Elizabeth.[23]

Maxwell's conclusions reflected the stereotypes held by his nonsouthern informants rather than the actual characteristics of the white southern migrants. Donald Janson, a Chicago news reporter who found "the hillbilly problem" worthy of a feature story in 1963, was more perceptive. He recognized that the label "hillbilly" was applied to *all* working-class white southerners, not just to the mountaineers who constituted only a portion of the migrant population. Nor did he propose that either the white southerners or the English constituted a race. He wrote:

> The newcomers are hill folk and flatlanders displaced at home by automation in the mines and mechanization of the farms.
> Thousands of these unskilled laborers, fewer than half of them true hillbillies, have arrived in the last few years. Few have found permanent jobs. The influx has been going on for some years, but it has accelerated in the last eight years, officials said.[24]

Janson estimated that there were 30,000 white southerners concentrated in a small area of Chicago on the North Side, centered on Wilson Avenue and Broadway. He found that other Chicagoans attributed a number of objectionable characteristics to the group: throwing garbage in the street, sexual immorality, lack of appreciation for education or religion,

wife-beating, and knife-fighting. In a sympathetic vein he
did state, "The poverty-stricken southerners, often unable to
read or write, were cruelly victimized." That these people
were labeled and derided as an undesirable minority group
is indicated in his declaration: "The term 'hillbilly' has been
applied so derisively here that it is now resented as much as
the Negroes resent 'nigger.' "

In 1964 William Braden and Morton Kondracke wrote two
articles on the hillbillies for the Chicago *Sun-Times*.[25] They
ascribed what they regarded as Chicago's newest minority
problem to the heavy influx of whites from Appalachia,
summing it up in these words:

> Others have come, too, in recent years. Mexicans and
> Puerto Ricans, Eskimos and American Indians. But
> Southern whites have constituted the bulk of the in-
> flux, and a majority of these have come from Appalachia.

Braden and Kondracke revealed that the white southerners
constituted enough of a social problem to be the object of
special welfare programs conducted by the Cook County
Department of Public Aid, the Col. Robert R. McCormick
Boys Club, Hull House, and the Mayor's Commission on
Youth Welfare. These writers explicitly compared the white
southerners to the black minority, quoting the statement of a
social worker:

> Like the Southern white population, the city's Negro
> population consists primarily of rural migrants who have
> come up here from the South. And to some extent, the
> difficulties both groups have encountered have common
> roots.
> Of course the two examples aren't completely similar.
> There is no doubt that color is responsible for ignorant
> prejudice and for some of the discrimination that is
> practiced against the Negro.
> But the Southern whites are discriminated against,
> too. And their color has nothing to do with it. They are
> discriminated against because they are rural people whose
> ways and mannerisms seem foreign to an urban people.

The White Southern Laborer as Hillbilly

It may be true, as some of the writers quoted above contend, that the influx of white southern workers into northern cities has greatly increased since about 1952 or 1953. (See appendix, Table 8, for migration of white southerners to nonsouthern cities 1955–60.) However, the phenomenon of the working-class white southern minority, labeled as hillbillies, stereotyped, and discriminated against in the northern city, is not new. A few early sociological studies showed that working-class white southerners were concentrated in certain areas of northern cities in the 1930s. These southerners were regarded by others as a distinct ethnic group, and they also regarded themselves in this manner. Furthermore, these studies and later census data confirm that the term hillbilly is applied to all working-class white southern migrants, not just to mountaineers, as picturesquely described by Maxwell. There is evidence that in Cincinnati, just across the border from eastern Kentucky, most of the so-called hillbillies are indeed from the Appalachian mountains.[26] In Detroit and Chicago only a minority are.

In 1938 Erdmann D. Beynon studied white southern laborers in Flint, Michigan, and concluded that the people with whom the migrants came into contact treated them as a single homogeneous group regardless of the part of the South from which they came.[27] The result, he noted, was an emergent group consciousness among the white southerners. About the same time Elmer Akers and Amos Hawley, of the University of Michigan, studied white southern workers in Detroit.[28] Both Akers and Hawley found that the migrants were concentrated in certain neighborhoods, even though their density was insufficient to constitute segregation. The clusters of white southern workers were usually located in neighborhoods near factories or lines of cheap transportation.

Even before 1940 Akers found that white southern workers in Detroit were called hillbillies, although the terms "briar-hopper" and "ridgerunner" were also used. Like Beynon, he found that hillbilly was used to describe any working-class white southerner, not just mountaineers. He noted also a fact that is repeatedly obscured by the association of the term hillbilly with mountain folk. This fact is that while the states of Kentucky and Tennessee contribute most of the white migrants to the North Central states, not all and perhaps not even half of the migrants are from the mountainous areas of these or other southern states. Akers declared, "We met a few of the southern highlanders but their number in Detroit is small."[29]

As recently as 1960, census data showed that mountaineers still did not predominate among white southern migrants to Chicago and Detroit despite a widespread impression to the contrary.[30] Of nearly 20,000 who migrated from Tennessee to Illinois between 1955 and 1960 (of whom 71 percent went to the Chicago area), only 30 percent came from the Appalachian counties of the eastern part of the state. One lowland area in the Mississippi valley, including the city of Memphis, contributed a higher proportion (35 percent) of the migrants than did the entire Appalachian area. Of the white migrants from Kentucky to Illinois only 20 percent were from Appalachian counties. A somewhat higher proportion of white migrants who came to Michigan from Tennessee and Kentucky were from the southern Appalachians, 42 and 46 percent respectively. Nevertheless, over half of the migrants still came from other parts of the two states.

Yet the stereotype of the hillbilly definitely includes the notion that he is a mountaineer, a white southerner whose caricature is to be seen in Snuffy Smith of the comic strip. It may be that the growing prosperity of the urban South and the continued poverty of southern Appalachia has caused some increase in the proportion of highlanders among white southern migrants. It is clear, however, that the term hillbilly is applied indiscriminately to working-class white southerners in many northern cities. Although the backgrounds of the migrants from the cities and farms of the lowlands and those from isolated mountain hamlets differ, their experiences as migrants are nevertheless quite similar.

A Case Study in Chicago

Between 1947 and 1949 the author made a case study of a hillbilly colony on the west side of Chicago.[31] Although the findings reflect conditions prevailing twenty years ago, subsequent reports, such as the news stories from Chicago quoted previously, indicate that neither the stereotype nor the problems of the white southerners have changed, unless they have changed in the direction of a more exaggerated stereotype and more difficult problems.

The settlement studied by the author was neither the first nor the last white southern colony to exist in Chicago. In 1929 Vivien Palmer discovered such a colony in an industrialized section of the North Side. Palmer wrote of the concentration, the problems, and the adjustment of the white southerners:

> Families have crowded together in order to meet the high rents and the crises of unemployment, and in this section single dwellings often house two or three families.
>
> A large frame building at Wolfram and Lincoln streets is looked upon as the headquarters of the colony and is managed by a young Tennesseean who came to the city about six years ago. Here the new arrival can find lodging, secure information about jobs, receive his mail until he has a permanent address, meet his pals, and exchange the latest gossip from home for news about his Chicago friends.[32]

In 1949, twenty years later, old residents of the area still remembered this colony with displeasure. One said of the founder, a young merchant from western Tennessee (not the mountains):

> He just tried to put too many Tennessee people in a house he'd rent. He filled the whole house up and then put them in the garages—that was when people ran him out of the neighborhood! There wasn't but one or two toilets in the whole place, for forty or fifty people, and it got to where they were using the yard for a toilet.

Another neighbor said: "Those places were ruining the neighborhood, running the property down. This ain't a rooming-house neighborhood—most of the people live in one- or two-family houses."

By 1947 this colony had disappeared because of neighborhood antagonism, but many others existed throughout the city. Seven areas were identified in which white southerners were a noticeable element in the population in the sense that they were present in sufficient numbers for other persons to be aware of their presence through personal contact. One of these colonies was the one on the North Side that Chicago news reporters featured in 1963 as the largest hillbilly area in the city.

The area chosen for the author's study, however, was one on the Near West Side between Ashland and Kedzie Streets, just south of Madison Street. The white southerners who lived there have long since been displaced by blacks and Puerto Ricans. During World War II and for a few years thereafter, however, Madison Street was dotted with hillbilly taverns similar to those on the North Side described in 1963 by Donald Janson:

> The sign outside advertised "country music" until 4 A.M. Inside rangy musicians with Southern accents twanged guitars and sang "K-E-N-T-U-C-K-Y—it spells Kentucky, but it means paradise."[33]

The white migrants who lived near the West Side taverns were mostly from the upper South. Public school records showed that Tennessee predominated as their state of origin, with three rural counties in the flatlands of western Tennessee being particularly well represented. One short street in the area was often called "Tennessee Street," reflecting the tendency of the migrants to settle in clusters according to the state and even the county from which they had migrated.

The factors that led to this clustering were the same as those that influenced the pattern of settlement of foreign ethnic groups in American cities. One factor was very social —the operation of the grapevine. Successive newcomers would find their first lodging with "pioneers" from their own communities in the South and would often find permanent residences in the same neighborhood. The other factor was impersonal—the characteristics of the area, including the availability of cheap, furnished rooms, proximity to some factories, and access to others by public transportation. Irish and Italian immigrants had settled in this "port of entry" before the white southerners; blacks and Puerto Ricans acquired the neighborhood after they left.

White southerners most frequently found employment as semiskilled or unskilled laborers. Although some of the migrants had finished high school, most had not. Nearly all had moved to Chicago in search of work. Few, however, had put down deep roots in Chicago. Families who had migrated twelve to fifteen years previously were likely to have returned to the South two or three times for periods of residence up to a year, and briefer visits were frequent. Identification with the home community was sustained by this pattern of going back and forth.

These people were called hillbillies and were highly conscious of the unfavorable connotations of the name. Some thought it incongruous because it implied that they came from the mountains. All resented it because of its insulting implication that they were "poor white trash." No one knows just how the term came to be used in this particular way. White southerners who had lived in the Near West Side as early as 1925 contended that they were called hillbillies even then. As previously noted, the most likely explanation is that the term derived from the widespread assumption that most white southerners do come from the hills and hollows of the southern Appalachians. In addition, the commercialization of hillbilly music serves to sustain the usage. Like the hillbillies themselves, the music is not an unalloyed product of the mountains. It is a modern, commercial product that bears little resemblance to the folk ballads of the southern highlands. The popularity of hillbilly music and hillbilly taverns with working-class white southerners serves to brand all of them as hillbillies.

The Stereotype of the Hillbilly

The southern accent was the primary identifying mark of the hillbilly; the term had a definite regional connotation. Not surprisingly, some migrants from the southern sections of Missouri and Illinois found themselves mistaken for southerners. The term also suggested that those to whom it was applied had a rural origin; this connotation persists in later descriptions of the hillbillies. Most important, it had a definite class connotation. Native Chicagoans who were questioned as to what kind of people would be called hillbillies replied with such terms as "poor white trash," "slum people from the South," and "unskilled workers."

The traits considered typical of the white southern migrants were similar to those found in the stereotypes of many other minority groups. The white southerners were often compared to such ethnic groups as the Italians and the Poles for their "clannishness." A restaurant owner exclaimed, "The southern people may be the most sociable people in the world in the South, but when they get up here they get clannish!" Low standards of hygiene and sanitation were ascribed to them— a few northerners really believed that the white southerners were unaccustomed to wearing shoes. More serious and more widespread was the belief that they lived in filth. A realtor went so far as to say, "They'd just as soon use the floor for a toilet as go to the bathroom. We'd rather rent to a Negro, a Mexican, or a Filipino than to a white person from the South."

There was a widespread belief that the moral standards of the southern migrants were equally low; police officers especially were convinced of this. Heavy drinking and brawling were believed to be common among the men. Considered even more objectionable was an alleged proclivity for knife-fighting. Akers had found this element of the stereotype in Detroit, quoting a northern woman who said: "Even though the Syrians and Armenians are themselves pretty handy with the knife, they are afraid of the southerners."[34] In Chicago the white southern laborers were often likened to blacks in this respect.

One bartender made the comparison an unfavorable one for the white southerners:

> These hillbillies fight a lot, and they use knives when they do. Chicago fellows don't fight that way. It's just not natural. Now all the niggers carry knives. It's different when a nigger uses a knife—they're just niggers and they ain't even human. But a white man is a human!

Another type of behavior sometimes attributed to the white southern minority was still regarded as typical in 1956, according to James Maxwell. This is incest. In his article in *The Reporter* Maxwell quoted a police officer who said:

> Incest is another matter which a lot of mountaineers see differently than we do. They usually come from small, isolated communities where there's a considerable amount of inbreeding anyway, and they can't see why it's any business of the police what they do with their sex life.[35]

Of greatest practical consequence to the white southern workers was their reputation for mobility or shiftlessness. There was some foundation for this impression but the degree of mobility was exaggerated. Employers, school teachers, and church workers, in particular, believed that the southerners were constantly moving back and forth between Chicago and the South. They were regarded as drifters, not as stable, solid, reliable citizens and workers. This led to the major form of discrimination against this native white minority group—treatment of the workers as a marginal segment of the labor force.

Discrimination Against White Southerners

The period of the author's study was one of high employment, so few of the migrants failed in their quest for work. Yet in seven of fourteen industrial plants studied, officials stated openly that they would hire white southern workers only when they could not get anybody else. The main reason they gave was the unreliability of the southern workers. Some said, however, that laziness, lack of education and skills, and an overdeveloped spirit of independence made them undesirable as employees.

In those plants in which the migrants were regarded more favorably, their position was still marginal. The foremen and the skilled workers were not southerners and many were Italian Americans—"foreigners" in the eyes of the white southerners. Only a few white southern workers had advanced into positions in which they could not be easily and quickly replaced. Even the officials of three plants that employed relatively large numbers of white southerners regarded them as a pool of unskilled, not-too-apt, undependable workers whose chief asset was their availability when demands for labor were high. The operation of the grapevine created this asset. When a plant was hiring, the word would quickly get back to southern communities. During World War II some employers with defense contracts even found that they could avoid hiring black workers without giving evidence of racial discrimination. They simply kept their positions filled with whites by utilizing this informal recruiting mechanism.

Friction between white southerners and other workers was minimal. Most of that which existed arose from personal encounters in which the term hillbilly was used as an epithet. As has been indicated, occasionally a white southerner would find that a flat or a furnished room had "just been rented" when the landlord heard his southern accent. The type of place in which discrimination, though subtle, was most consistent and in which conflict with nonsoutherners was most likely to occur was the tavern. Tavern owners who wanted the hillbilly trade systematically enticed it. Those who did not made it evident by their demeanor that white southerners were not welcome, and were quick to call the police if a hillbilly became boisterous.

The Hillbilly Tavern

The activities that gave the white southerners their highest visibility as a group took place in the hillbilly taverns and, paradoxically, in the churches. In the case of the latter, a minority of the migrants attended storefront churches of various "holiness" sects. The shouting, the spirited singing, and the twanging of guitars and banjos impinged harshly on the ear of even the casual passerby. To many urban Americans, particularly Roman Catholics, the sounds of "the old-time religion" were alien and unpleasant.

"A joyful noise" emanated from the hillbilly tavern, too, but the fights that sometimes spilled out onto the sidewalk evoked horror and disgust from witnesses. Quiet except for the jukebox during the day, after dark these taverns were filled with the whine of electric guitars and the nasal tones of country singers. There was no floor show—the patrons were the show. Drinking cheap beer, dancing, talking with kindred spirits from the South, occasionally fighting among themselves or with Yankees who invaded their turf, the migrants found escape from the impersonality of urban living in a true ethnic tavern.

Entrepreneurs, few of them white southerners themselves, recognized the profit to be made from catering to this group. The image of the hillbilly tavern was most clearly expressed in a description by a bartender of how a tavern owner who had accumulated a stake by running such an establishment changed to the even more profitable night club trade:

> Our original place, down the street, was a real hillbilly tavern. We even had an old wagon in there, with a fellow sitting up on the seat playing a guitar. Those hillbillies would raise hell in there.
>
> We used to have hillbillies in here, too, but the boss changed that. We don't have them in here now. We cater to a high-class trade now—people that will spend a lot of money. We don't have any hillbilly music in here, and we took out the dance floor. We stopped serving "shorty" bottles of beer and draught beer. Something else we've cut out is the fights. You can't have those in a high class place. You get a big place like this, and you have some bouncers walking around keeping things quiet. If somebody starts a fight, out he goes. But in these little places like the one we used to have, you don't have anybody like that. The hillbillies come in there and drink

fifteen-cent beer and fight. And they holler at everybody —holler at the bartender, holler at the orchestra, holler at each other!

Then, as now, the hillbilly tavern was important to white southern, working-class migrants for two reasons. First, it served as a gathering place where white southerners could enjoy informal, intimate associations with companions who shared similar backgrounds and common experiences as migrants. At the same time, however, the existence of these taverns reinforced the stereotype of the white southern migrant as a "hard-drinking, feudin', fightin' hillbilly" and these taverns came to be known as "the place to find southerners."

Reactions of White Southerners as a Minority

It would not be easy for the so-called hillbillies to forget that they were southerners even if they were inclined to do so. As part of the ethnic mosaic of a working-class area of a northern city, their group identity is reinforced. In a part of Chicago in which in 1947 most people were conscious of being Italian, Polish, Irish, and the like, the southerners soon concluded that nobody was just "an American." They thus came to compare themselves with other "nationalities," sometimes even referring to themselves, the Italians, and other white groups as belonging to different races. In the manner of other ethnic minorities, they came to refer to themselves as hillbillies but were quick to take offense if a nonsoutherner used the label.

Their group consciousness was defensive in nature. While they felt that they were a minority that was discriminated against in Chicago, they felt themselves to be superior to, and essentially more American than, most of the rest of the population. Some of them even accepted their reputation for fighting as evidence that "southern people are proud people." A story that many white southerners told about themselves reflects their defensiveness about their status in Chicago. It ran like this:

This fellow kept making cracks about my being a hill-billy. I didn't say nothing about it for a while, but I finally got tired of it. So I said to him, "Listen, I've always heard there was just two kinds of people." He fell for it and came back, "Yeah? What are the two kinds?" I really had him then! I told him, "There's a hillbilly and there's a son of a bitch. I'm a hillbilly. What are you?"

A common reaction of minority group members is to make intragroup distinctions. In this case, some members regard others as an embarrassment to the entire group. Some white southerners in Chicago thus distinguished between "good" and "bad" hillbillies. Those who did not frequent the taverns (and many did not) regarded the habitués of such establishments as a disgrace to the whole group. These "good" hillbillies were aware of the fact that they were members of an identifiable group and that the behavior of some members would reflect unfavorably on all.

The Durability of the Hillbilly Minority

Yet the upwardly mobile white southerner could easily escape from the hillbilly minority. The white southern migrant who could afford to move to a somewhat higher class suburb or part of the city could thereby reduce the salience of his southern background. In the author's research, some such "climbers" were located in other sections of Chicago. Many others looked forward to moving out someday.

Nevertheless, working-class white southern minorities have existed in Chicago, Detroit, and other northern cities for nearly half a century now. Although the individuals who compose the minority change over the years, the group remains, visible and self-conscious. Part of its durability stems from the attitude of some of the members, who feel that their stay in the northern city is not a permanent one. Unlike foreign immigrants, they find it easy to go back home periodically; this mobility tends to preclude their assimilation into northern white society. More important, there are no immigration laws to restrict the flow of successive waves of newcomers into the white southerners' neighborhoods. The much-vaunted assimilation of foreign ethnic groups has resulted in large part from the fact that the flow of "greenhorns" has been drastically restricted by immigration laws since World War I. The escape of individuals from the foreign immigrant community meant that the visible portion of the minority was constantly being reduced. Like the nation's other new minority, the Puerto Ricans, white southerners are free to replenish the hillbilly neighborhood as rapidly as earlier migrants disappear into the general white population. Until the South offers all its children, white and black, educational and employment opportunities equal to those provided in other regions, there will be a hillbilly minority outside the South.

The Affluent Migrant

The hillbilly "problem" is fundamentally an economic one. The fact that these people have a visibility as white southerners is important primarily because they are poor and because, like other disadvantaged newcomers, they are channeled by social and economic forces into identifiable areas of settlement. In such neighborhoods the entire group, the majority of whom constitute part of the human wealth that the South can ill afford to lose, are stereotyped as "po' white trash" because of the behavior of a small number.

What of white southern migrants who are not poor, who are invited to other regions to take salaried positions, who rent spacious apartments or buy houses in the suburbs? Do they quickly forget their southern heritage? Are they allowed to forget it?

These relatively affluent migrants do not become a cohesive, group-conscious minority like the hillbillies, but neither do they forget that they are southerners. The discrimination they encounter is mild and highly personal. They have a sense of being different, but their experience is that of the isolated stranger, not that of a member of an alien minority. As long as they retain their southern accents they are likely to be reminded of their origin in ways that are often amusing but sometimes infuriating.

It is amusing to be asked by a stranger, "Aren't you from Georgia? I know a fellow from Atlanta who talks just like you do." If the white southerner can laugh at himself, he can find humor in the look of bewilderment on the face of a Yankee listener when he uses words such as "war" (waa-ah) or "beer" (bee-ah). The varieties of reactions of nonsoutherners to the subject of grits and their mystification at the term "pot likker" can also be diverting.

Not so amusing, particularly to the "liberated" white southerner, is the stereotyping of white southerners as being uniformly bigoted in matters of race. Sometimes the northern or western white is as prejudiced in his own way as the meanest "cracker." He may welcome the white southerner as a kindred spirit and immediately ascribe to him the very attitudes that the southerner has renounced. Even the strongly prejudiced southerner may be angered at expressions of prejudice by nonsoutherners, because he feels they reveal the hypocrisy inherent in northern denunciations of southern racial practices.

The reaction of some self-conscious liberals outside the South leaves the white southerner in a state of impotent rage. Willie Morris describes this sort of encounter:

> Three or four times, on friendly occasions, some agitated native would flush me for being a white Southerner; once a long-legged Eastern bluestocking with Gauloises smoke curling out of her ample nostrils blamed me for the institution of slavery, the Compromise of 1877, the Jim Crow laws, and the riots in Watts, and ended up, after two more drinks, identifying me as "poor white trash."[36]

Many white southerners are not anxious to forget or to conceal their background. Some may attempt to erase the traces of the southern accent; others find the accent ineradicable and do not care. Gerald W. Johnson, who regarded white southerners as one of America's minorities, observed:

Yet I have never encountered a white Southerner without pride in his heritage. Some no doubt exist, but they are invisible, presumably because they conceal their Southern nativity. For the rest, the danger in which they stand is not that of losing their pride of birth but that of permitting it to swell into a foolish and offensive arrogance. Men whom ambition, or economic or professional necessity, drove out of the South decades ago still tend to proclaim, rather than to conceal, their origin. Even those who fled from the intellectual sterility of their early environment realize that its emotional wealth is prodigious; they may be able to think better almost anywhere else, but nowhere else can they feel as intensely, so they are aware that their voluntary exile is far from being one hundred per cent gain.[37]

The ears of white southerners are attuned to the southern accent in all its varieties. The southerner can not only tell that another person is from the South, but he can also make a pretty good guess as to whether the speaker is from the Deep South, the Upper South, Tidewater Virginia, Charleston, or Savannah. Amid strangers with whom it is an effort to make conversation, the exiles often gravitate to each other, for they can easily find something to talk about. James M. Dabbs describes this reaction:

A friend who has lived in several parts of the country tells me there is one sure mark of the Southerner; his first question is, "Where're you from?" If you reply: "Well . . I hardly know. There was San Francisco, and Omaha, and . . ." his expression changes and you become to him, if anything, a slightly strange being, perhaps interesting because strange, but not one of the folks. But if you're from the South, who knows? With all his family connections, you might be kin to him.[38]

In addition to playing the game "Do you know . . . ?" with both people and places, white southerners can find many other things to talk about. One topic is why each left the South. Sometimes the inhospitality of nonsoutherners, undoubtedly greatly exaggerated, becomes the focus of discussion. The legendary hospitality of the South becomes magnified in reminiscence. Another favorite subject is where to find southern foods. Okra, collards, mustard greens, grits, black-eyed peas, turnip greens, and hush-puppy mix are regional specialties that the southern cook must search for diligently outside the homeland. Some grocers have never heard of many of these delicacies. The author was once advised to look for hushpuppies in a shoe store! When asked if he had okra an Italian vegetable vendor in Chicago replied with a sneer, "Hell, no! That's nigger food!" And in truth the question of food reminds the white southerner of his historic relationship to black southerners. Morris writes:

> At Al Murray's apartment in Harlem, on New Year's Day 1967, the Murrays, the [Ralph] Ellisons, and the Morrises congregated for an unusual feast: bourbon, collard greens, black-eyed peas, ham-hocks, and cornbread —a kind of ritual for all of us. Where else in the East but in Harlem could a Southern white boy greet the New Year with the good-luck food he had had as a child, and feel at home as he seldom had thought he could in the Cave?[39]

If the conversation between white southerners continues for long the subject of race almost invariably arises. The misconceptions of other Americans about black-white relations in the South and the hypocrisy of dwellers in lily-white suburbs who criticize the South for its segregation are balm to the wounds of southern pride. Even exiled white southern liberals may end up defending the South to each other, just as they find themselves defending it to outsiders whose image of the region is a hateful caricature. No one except the black southerner knows the evils of southern racism as well as the liberal white southerner, but no one else knows as well how a complex situation has been oversimplified by people who have never lived in it. In Morris' words:

> In America, perhaps more than any other place, and in the South perhaps more than any other region, we go back to our home in dreams and memories, hoping it

remains what it was on a lazy, still summer's day twenty years ago—and yet our sense of it is forever violated by others who see it, not as home, but as the dark side of hell.[40]

White Southern Pride

Most white southerners do not carry with them the feeling of the superiority of their homeland that seems to characterize many natives of California, Boston, and even New York City. They are quick to apologize for it. If they are hillbillies, they almost certainly have known hard times there and cannot forget that they left because life in their native region seemed to lead to a dead end. If they are well-educated and affluent, they are aware that the cultural and economic horizons of the region are not yet as high as those of other parts of the United States. If they are liberal, they grieve for the South's sins of prejudice and they know the oppression of the closed society. Yet all have some good memories of old times there and they know that their homeland is not the dark side of hell. The pride of a white southerner is that of a member of a minority group who knows that he must strain to argue the superiority or even the equality of his folk, but who is not ready to renounce his heritage.

Notes

[1] Hal Bruno, "Chicago's Hillbilly Ghetto," *The Reporter,* June 4, 1964, p. 28.

[2] R. A. Schermerhorn, *These Our People* (Boston: Heath, 1949), p. 7.

[3] Carter Goodrich, *Migration and Economic Opportunity* (Philadelphia: University of Pennsylvania Press, 1936); John N. Webb and Malcolm J. Brown, *Migrant Families* (Washington, D.C.: Works Project Administration, 1938); Warren S. Thompson, *Research Memorandum on Internal Migration in the Depression* (New York: Social Science Research Council, Bulletin No. 30, 1937); W. Parker Mauldin, "Selective Migration from Small

Towns," *American Sociological Review*, 5 (October 1940), 749–758; Gilbert A. Sanford, "Selective Migration in a Rural Alabama Community," *American Sociological Review*, 5 (October 1940), 759–766.

4 Henry S. Shryock, Jr., and Charles B. Nam, "Educational Selectivity of Interregional Migration," *Social Forces*, 43 (March 1965), 299–310.

5 James S. Brown and George A. Hillery, Jr., "The Great Migration, 1940–1960," in Thomas R. Ford (ed.), *The Southern Appalachian Region: A Survey* (Lexington: University of Kentucky Press, 1962), p. 77.

6 *Ibid.*, p. 68.

7 Shyrock and Nam, *op. cit.*, p. 309.

8 Howard W. Odum, *Southern Regions of the United States* (Chapel Hill: University of North Carolina Press, 1936), p. 471.

9 H. L. Mencken, *A Mencken Chrestomathy* (New York: Knopf, 1967), pp. 184–196.

10 *Ibid.*, pp. 184–185.

11 *Ibid.*, p. 193.

12 Russell W. Middleton, "Racial Problems and the Recruitment of Academic Staff at Southern Colleges and Universities," *American Sociological Review*, 26 (December 1961), 960–970.

13 *Ibid.*, p. 965.

14 *Ibid.*, p. 968.

15 Willie Morris, *North Toward Home* (Boston: Houghton Mifflin, 1967), pp. 319–320.

16 *Ibid.*, p. 347.

17 The term "hillbilly" will be used in this chapter as a short-hand expression for "working-class, white, southern migrants." This is the way it is used in many northern cities, sometimes by the white southerners themselves. It must be recognized, however, that it is a derogatory group label and is usually resented by the people to whom it is applied, particularly if the speaker is not part of their group.

18 Dale Nouse, "Detroiters Like City Just Fine, Survey Reveals," Detroit *Free Press*, 1952 (exact date not available).

19 Louis Adamic, "The Hill-Billies Come to Detroit," *The Nation*, 140 (February 13, 1935), 177–178.

20 Henry Hill Collins, *America's Own Refugees* (Princeton, N.J.: Princeton University Press, 1941), p. 26.

21 Alfred M. Lee and Norman D. Humphrey, *Race Riot* (New York: Dryden, 1943), p. 91.

22 James A. Maxwell, "Down from the Hills and into the Slums," *The Reporter*, December 13, 1956, p. 27.

23 *Ibid.*, p. 28.

24 Donald Janson, "Displaced Southerners Find Chicago an Impersonal Haven," *The New York Times*, August 31, 1963.

25 William Braden and Morton Kondracke, "Mountain Folk Adrift in Our City," and "What City Is Doing for Hill Folk," Chicago *Sun-Times* (February 9 and 10, 1964).

26 See Roscoe Giffin, "Appalachian Newcomers in Cincinnatti," in Ford, *The Southern Appalachian Region, op. cit.*, pp. 79–84.

27 Erdmann D. Beynon, "The Southern White Laborer Migrates to Michigan," *American Sociological Review*, 3 (June 1938), 333–345.

28 Elmer Akers, "Southern Whites in Detroit" (unpublished report, Bureau of Government, University of Michigan, n.d.), and Amos H. Hawley, Jr., "The Mobility of the Southern Immigrant in Detroit" (unpublished report, Bureau of Government, University of Michigan, June 1937).

29 Akers, *op. cit.*, p. 6.

30 Based on *United States Census of Population: 1960*, Final Report PC(2) 2B, "Mobility for States and State Economic Areas" (Washington, D.C.: Government Printing Office, 1963), Tables 35 and 36.

31 Lewis M. Killian, "Southern White Laborers in Chicago's West Side" (unpublished Ph.D. dissertation, University of Chicago, 1949).

32 Vivien M. Palmer, *Social Backgrounds of Chicago's Local Communities* (Chicago: Local Community Research Committee, University of Chicago, 1930).

33 Janson, *op. cit.*

34 Akers, *op. cit.*, p. 74.

35 Maxwell, *op. cit.*, p. 28.

36 Morris, *op. cit.*, p. 404.

37 Gerald W. Johnson, *The Man Who Feels Left Behind* (New York: Morrow, 1961), pp. 67–68.

38 James M. Dabbs, *The Southern Heritage* (New York, Knopf, 1958), p. 26.

39 Morris, *op. cit.*, p. 387.

40 *Ibid.*, pp. 380–381.

Chapter 6 ◉ White Southerners in a Pluralistic America

C. Vann Woodward, a white southern historian who sees the faults of the South clearly but who never ceases to search for the worthwhile elements of its heritage, has written:

> The South was American a long time before it was Southern in any self-conscious or distinctive way. It remains more American by far than anything else, and has all along. After all, it fell the lot of one Southerner from Virginia to define America. The definition he wrote in 1776 voiced aspirations that were rooted in his native region before the nation was born.[1]

White southerners have always been near the center of the stage in the drama of American history. Although New England Yankees fired the first shots of the Revolution, the South furnished both the father of the country and the author of the Declaration of Independence. Thomas Jefferson purchased the Louisiana Territory and Andrew Jackson drove the last British invaders from the soil of the United States. When the nation cast hungry eyes on more territory west of the Mississippi, white southerners gave enthusiastic support to the expansion of the empire. They led in the settlement of Texas. Numerous young officers who would later become Confederate generals first became American heroes in the U.S. Army blue during the Mexican War. During both world wars the South earned the reputation of being as patriotic as any region and more militaristic than the rest of the nation. In peacetime white southerners were one of the key elements of Franklin D. Roosevelt's coalition, and modern Republican leaders have recognized that their party cannot retain national power without splitting the once solidly Democratic South and keeping it split. George Wallace is unmistakably a southern politician, but he attempts to escape this narrow identification by bidding his followers, "Stand Up for America."

Southern Fundamentalism

The Americanism of white southerners, however, has not been inspired by the spirit of diversity and change characteristic of a nation of immigrants. Like their religion, the Americanism of white southerners has a fundamentalist tone. It looks more to the past than to the future for a model of what America should be or might have been. Hence, as currents of change have swept the nation, the South has appeared as the most recalcitrant region, repeatedly blocking the achievement of some new national consensus.

When, after the Revolution, the farmers of New England turned from the plow to the factory, white southerners fought the tariffs passed to aid the new industries and insisted that agriculture was the true basis of the nation's prosperity. A century later, even after America had become the industrial colossus of the world, a school of southern writers called the Agrarians were still arguing that the agrarian way was morally superior to the industrial way that was sweeping the nation. When the rest of the nation was ready to abandon slavery, the South seceded rather than give up the institution. Indeed, the white southerners insisted that it was *they* who were faithful to the spirit and the letter of the Constitution, and that it was their enemies, who sought to compel them to remain in a union that they had entered voluntarily and to accept changes to which they had never agreed, who had forsaken it. When, in 1954, the United States Supreme Court declared racial segregation unconstitutional, ninety-six congressmen and senators from southern states issued a manifesto charging that the court had deserted constitutional principles and substituted naked power for the established law of the land.

Pierre van den Berghe has characterized the United States as a *"Herrenvolk* democracy," a system in which egalitarian ideals are applied only to "the people"—in this case, the whites—and one that is democratic for the master race but tyrannical for subordinate groups.[2] He argues that this description of the republic has been accurate since its birth and that only a few idealists interpreted the Declaration of Independence literally to apply to all people. The Constitution, he says, "was a conservative document, a compact between the northern bourgeoisie and the southern slave-owning aristocracy."[3] When the nation was founded, to most whites "people" meant "whites."

To a greater extent than citizens in any other region, white southerners have clung unabashedly and stubbornly to this primitive, fundamental meaning of Americanism. They have not been alone in their practice of discrimination against Americans who are not of the white *herrenvolk*, but they have been less ready to pay lip service to redefinitions of the meaning of Americanism and democracy. For this the white South has paid the price of being "a moral lightning rod, a deflector of national guilt, a scapegoat for stricken conscience. It has served the country much as the Negro has served the white supremacist—as a floor under self-esteem."[4] Even the deviant white southern liberal has suffered this penalty, for while he has recognized the need for radical change in the South and in the rest of the nation, he has lacked the glib confidence of many reformers that such change could come easily.

The Revival of Pluralism

Although they have consistently proclaimed their fundamental Americanism, white southerners have been uneasy partners in the federal union. They have cherished their regional identity, found reason for pride in even minor cultural differences, and been reluctant to disappear into a homogeneous American people. In this sense they have resisted what Milton Gordon has identified as a powerful ideological trend in the kind of society the United States has become:

In the modern industrialized urban state, such an ideological model, stemming from classic eighteenth and nineteenth century liberalism blended with nationalism, views the huge nation as "the people"; the remnants of former types of ethnicity are then regarded as inconvenient vestiges—to be tolerated, if the state is democratic—but not to be encouraged.[5]

In recent years Gordon and other social scientists have pointed out that, the white South and its black minority aside, assimilation has not advanced as far in American society as its advocates believe. Gordon argues:

The United States . . . is a multiple melting pot in which acculturation for all groups beyond the first generation of immigrants, without eliminating all value conflicts, has been massive and decisive, but in which structural separation on the basis of race and religion—structural pluralism, as we have called it—emerges as the dominant sociological condition.[6]

At the same time social scientists have been rediscovering pluralism as a social reality, some members of minority groups —particularly Mexican-Americans, Indians, and blacks—have been refurbishing it as a goal. This is most noticeable in the case of black Americans, who have long given the appearance of being the most assimilationist minority, but who have now produced one group of leaders who advocate pluralism or even secession as the means to real equality. The ideal of an undifferentiated American identity has lost much of its luster.

Pluralism represents the effort of a group to cope with the problem of preserving its distinctive, historical identity when the demands of national unity threaten to override subsocietal loyalties. In equal measure it constitutes the effort of a subgroup to maintain the power to protect its own self-defined interests in a society in which the rule of the majority, or of a dominant minority, denies "minority rights." As a self-conscious minority struggling with both of these problems, white southerners are the nation's oldest pluralists. It is ironic that black pluralists are exploring some of the same sources of minority protection that the South has tried.

The Quest for Minority Power

The most persistent and troublesome problem of democracy
is the protection of minority interests under majority rule.
Political rhetoric proclaims that in a democracy power belongs
to the people. To those citizens who find the political decisions
congenial, this proposition appears to be an obvious, uncom-
plicated truth. "The people" are *their* kind. The minority group
member, outvoted and overruled, sooner or later asks the
question, "To *which* people does power belong?" He sees the
people as a *plural* of groups with diverse interests. He thinks
not only of individual rights, commonly desired and univer-
sally beneficial regardless of subgroup membership, but also of
group rights, peculiar to groups with special problems and
special interests. The shift of the emphasis of the black protest movement from civil rights to Black Power reflected the
adoption by a significant number of black leaders of the
concept of group rights. This change constituted a rejection of
the notion that either majority rule or constitutional guarantees of individual civil liberties were sufficient to guarantee
justice to a minority. Black people as a group needed a powerful voice in the formulation of political decisions.

Although few of them seemed to recognize it, this was a
familiar theme to white southerners. They had called it "states
rights" as they had pursued the same goal of minority protection now sought by black Americans. Discussing the South as
a conscious minority during the period from 1787 until 1861,
Jesse T. Carpenter says of white southerners as a separate and
distinct group within the United States:

> This *united* people was a *minority* people, ever sub-
> jected in all branches of the national government to the
> potential control of those who lived north of the Mason
> and Dixon line. In every decade of the Union, the sec-
> tional distribution of population and of states consigned
> to the South a minority role in the central government.[7]

Carpenter has identified four sources of minority protection
that were tried in succession by the South. All of these have

some points of resemblance to proposals advanced by various black leaders over a century later for the protection of minority rights of their group. One great difference in the quest of the blacks and that of the white southerners casts its shadow over all these points of similarity. Black leaders seek the right to control their own lives and communities. To white southerners, "self-determination" or "southern rights" has meant control not only of their own affairs but also of the fate of black southerners.

Local Self-Government

The first source was the principle of local self-government. Even during the formulation and ratification of the Constitution, white southerners revealed their fear of a powerful central government responsive to a nonsouthern majority. The Tenth Amendment, which reserved to the states the powers not delegated to the United States by the Constitution, reflected this fear. During the early years of the republic the southern states fought against the federal tariff, the first Bank of the United States, the federal Alien and Sedition Acts, and the growing power of the Supreme Court as arbiter of the constitutionality of laws. The states clung tenaciously to their "right" to make their own laws governing slavery, to maintain their own state banks, and to regulate their own commerce. Within the states, strong county governments developed. At an early date in the nation's history the South displayed the attitude that law officers attempting to enforce the law of the land were alien intruders if the minority did not concur in the law. In 1793, after the Supreme Court had rendered a judgment against the state of Georgia on behalf of two citizens of South Carolina in the case of *Chisholm v. Georgia,* Georgia's house of representatives passed a bill declaring that any federal marshal who should attempt to collect the judgment would be "guilty of a felony and shall suffer death, without benefit of clergy, by being hanged."[8]

A theme advanced by some Black Power advocates today is "self-determination for black communities." Black control of black schools was a battle cry during the New York City school crisis of 1968. Black control of the economy of the ghetto is proclaimed as an essential ingredient of black self-government. The police are defined as an alien, oppressive force; in 1969, 46 percent of blacks in a national sample believed that "local police are harmful to Negro rights."[9] In some urban black communities vigilante forces have been formed to regulate the behavior of private citizens and sometimes to monitor the activities of "the Man's" police force. Demands have been made that only black policemen be assigned to black areas. Stokely Carmichael and Charles V. Hamilton summed up the spirit of black self-government in the statement: "We must begin to think of the black community as a base of organization to control institutions in that community."[10] Paradoxically, this theme is prevalent in black communities at a time when many white southerners feel that they and their forebears have been fighting a long, losing battle for local control of local institutions. Again it must be noted that to white southerners local control has meant *white* control of both white and black institutions.

The Principle of the Concurrent Majority

As early as 1830 white southern proponents of group rights began to despair of the effectiveness of local self-government as a source of minority protection. They then elaborated the more formal theory of the concurrent majority, which was enunciated most forcefully by John C. Calhoun. This theory held that the unrestrained rule of a numerical majority would lead not to justice, but to the tyranny of the majority; hence a weaker, minority section should have some veto over the actions of the majority. Calhoun suggested that:

> There should be . . . two executives instead of one, each representing a section and each having the power of veto over acts of Congress. A measure should be required to pass that body, not by the members voting as one body, but by the representatives of the two sections voting separately.[11]

Such a proposal was never to be taken seriously by the Congress, but the state of South Carolina attempted to implement the theory of the concurrent majority by its Ordinance of Nullification, passed in 1832 in opposition to federal tariff laws. This ordinance declared the unpopular laws null and void, not binding upon the state. The nullifiers reasoned that when a sovereign state, which had entered the federal union voluntarily, deemed that a law violated its constitutional rights, then the constitutional compact could be brought into question. The controversial law could be incorporated into the Constitution as an amendment, if three-fourths of the states concurred, and thus become the law of the land. If a dissident state still found the law odious, it could refuse to become a party to the new compact and resort to the ultimate expedient of secession.

The right of nullification was recognized neither by the Congress nor by a white southern president, Andrew Jackson. The tariffs were reduced in a political compromise but a "Force Bill" was enacted authorizing the President to employ the armed forces to carry out the law. The principle of the concurrent majority was not forgotten in the South, however. In 1956 and 1957 the legislatures of nine southern states appealed to it once again by passing resolutions of interposition declaring the Supreme Court's school desegregation decision null and void. They no longer talked of secession, but insisted that the ruling should be validated by the process of constitutional amendment before it became binding upon the states. Again their voice went unheeded, and this time federal marshals and troops went into some states to enforce the law.

Black Americans, who, unlike states, have no status as a political entity, have had no doctrine of "reserved powers" to which to appeal. A few black leaders have argued that blacks never consented to become citizens of the United States; instead, their citizenship was conferred—or imposed—upon them by the Fourteenth Amendment. As a numerical minority in what they perceive as a white racist society blacks have come to fear the tyranny of the majority as did white southerners of a previous century, even though for *very different reasons*. They are losing faith that a white majority will ever do what is best for black interests and are finding effective coalitions with whites more and more difficult to achieve. Some organizations, notably SNCC, have shown their kinship to the New Left by subscribing to the theory of "participatory democracy." Among the principles of this theory as advanced in the *Port Huron Statement* of SDS are: "That decision-making of basic social consequence be carried on by public groupings; that politics be seen positively, as the art of collectively creating an acceptable pattern of social relations . . ."[12]

With its idealistic emphasis on the development of laws from the bottom up and rejection of their imposition from above, participatory democracy has much in common with the principle of the concurrent majority. It has been characterized as "the new anarchism" because it proposes a veto power for the minority, no matter how small. For the democratic dogma, "the voice of the people is the voice of God," it substitutes Thoreau's justification for civil disobedience; "One man who is more right than his neighbors is already a majority of one."

From the practice of civil disobedience through the advocacy of participatory democracy and black proportional representation, protesting blacks have sought to exercise a veto over the tyranny of the majority. The veto available to them has been a negative sanction, the power to create social disruption. They have more than matched the bombast of southern legislative resolutions with the deadly seriousness of "putting their bodies on the line." Through sit-ins, marches, rent strikes, and ghetto insurrections, black protesters have proved that white society cannot continue with business as usual without the concurrence of the black minority. After the riots— or revolts—of 1964 to 1967, Charles Hamilton gave what amounts to a restatement of the principle of the concurrent majority:

> The revolts have been saying: "You see, we too have some modicum of power, if it's only the power to destroy, to disrupt." Like all power, this minority weapon is as useful in the fact of its *potential* threat as in its actual use. Therefore, given clear evidence, now, that black people are willing to destroy their oppressors' property,

to disrupt their normal business cycle, it may well be that the white decision-makers will be forced to view the relations between the races in different terms; the cards are *not* all stacked in their favor.[13]

Constitutional Guarantees

The third source of minority protection identified by Carpenter as having been used by the Old South appears as the one that a people confident of their moral and legal position would have invoked first. During the decade immediately preceding the Civil War the South relied most heavily on the principle of constitutional guarantees, partly because nullification had failed. The burning issue by that time was slavery, not tariffs. White southern slaveholders argued that the Constitution protected their right to hold slaves not only in their own states, but anywhere in the United States. As late as 1857 they received confirmation of their position from the Supreme Court in the Dred Scott decision. Only the fear that the new Republican party, victorious in the election of 1860, would lead the rest of the nation to change or to disregard the Constitution led the white South to abandon its fundamentalist faith in that document.

For black Americans in the twentieth century, the principle of constitutional guarantees was the first line of defense, rather than one of the last resorts in the battle for minority protection. Viewing the Constitution as a progressive rather than a conservative instrument, they went again and again to the Supreme Court seeking rulings that would make American democracy color-blind and would promote the welfare of black citizens through the protection of individual liberties. The Legal Defense and Education Fund of the NAACP proved to be a school for constitutional lawyers. Even SNCC, which in a few years would be preaching "independent black power, race pride, black dignity, and the third world," began as an organization described by Jack Newfield as: "A religious band of middle-class, rather square reformers, seeking only 'our rights.' . . . Their guiding spirit was not even Gandhi so much as the Bill of Rights, the 13th, 14th, and 15th Amendments, and the Holy Bible."[14]

Only after ten years of desperate struggle to achieve equality within the framework of constitutional guarantees did the black protest movement split into two wings, one of which proclaimed that "the institutions of the society (the courts, the traditional political parties, the police, the educational institutions) are no longer seen as willing or able to meet the pressing needs of a majority of black people."[15] The other wing, represented by such leaders as Bayard Rustin, A. Philip Randolph, and Roy Wilkins, still retained its faith in the principle of constitutional guarantees in spite of repeated disappointments. The two sets of leaders are engaged in a bitter struggle for the allegiance of the mass of black Americans.

Secession

The final, desperate source of protection of white southern rights was the principle of independence—secession. However, with the regional memory of failure and defeat still strong, not even the most reactionary white southern leaders advocated a return to this course when the right to maintain a segregated society came under attack. Some black leaders such as Milton Henry, of "the Republic of New Africa," have proposed, however, that the establishment of an independent black nation is the only solution for the black minority. Although few in number, they are deadly serious. Robert S. Browne, a black university professor and member of the executive of the 1967 Black Power Conference, has argued that "a formal partitioning of the United States into two totally separate and independent nations, one white and one black" is necessary to give blacks an identity of which they can be proud.[16] Integration, he contends, is not likely to be achieved and, if it were, it would constitute a sort of painless genocide. Bayard Rustin, long a fighter for integration, is one of several prominent Negro spokesmen who have denounced separatist proposals as "a frustrated reaction" and "reversism." He argues that the Negro middle class will never accept separatism and that raising lower-class blacks to a level at which integration will be a realistic goal for them is the immediate task. Rustin declares: "I believe that the fundamental mistake of the nationalist movement is that it does not comprehend that class ultimately is a more driving force than color, and that any effort to build a society for American Negroes that is based on color alone is doomed to failure."[17]

The dream of a black republic in five Deep South states has the same allure for black separatists that Martin Luther King, Jr.'s dream of an integrated society held for him. That even a small minority of blacks earnestly propose such a step indicates that American unity is as gravely threatened in 1969 as it was in 1859. The problem of minority protection under majority rule is as far from being solved as ever. White southerners continue their search for a solution, but it is black Americans who insist that the problem must be solved immediately.

Two Ways for White Southerners

The entire nation has reached another critical juncture in its long struggle to maintain diversity in unity. The phrase "polarization into two societies," alarming when first uttered in 1968 by the National Advisory Commission on Civil Disorders, has become worn and trite. Yet the crisis of integration versus separatism remains acute. The efforts of the civil rights movement to integrate the South into the nation and blacks into the South fell so far short of the mark that both the feasibility and the desirability of integration have been brought into question, particularly in the minds of many blacks. Yet there are still integrationists, both white and black, who cling to the hope the South will be integrated into a nation in which blacks are truly assimilated. Recognition that the problem of black integration is indeed national, not merely southern, leads to a redefinition of the courses open to white southerners.

One course is for them to take the lead in demonstrating that racial harmony can be achieved in spite of group differences. Liberal white southerners who refuse to accept the judgment of the southern historian Ulrich B. Phillips that the essence of southern tradition was "a common resolve indomitably maintained that the South shall be and remain a white man's country" believe most strongly that this way is open.[18] The other course is for white southerners, purged of their liberal compatriots, to be the leaders of a national movement that would make the *herrenvolk* principle a public virtue instead of a hidden vice.

THE WAY OF RECONCILIATION. Some characteristics of the South and its black population offer support for the belief that desegregation and, ultimately, integration might be achieved more easily in that region than in others. The overt, *de jure* nature of segregation in the South before 1954 made it more vulnerable to legal attack than the subtle, *de facto* segregation that has finally been exposed in northern cities. White southerners were forced to develop quickly ingenious devices for segregating surreptitiously at a time when all forms of discrimination were being subjected to intense scrutiny. Northern racists had long used such devices as the "private club" and the neighborhood school. Such subterfuges are now under attack in all regions; in the South they may be most vulnerable because of their nascent quality.

It may also be significant that the South lags behind the North and the Far West in the degree of massive, physical segregation of blacks. Relatively few southern communities lack a black population; the large cities are not moving as rapidly to having 50 percent black populations as are northern cities. If white southern school officials would commit themselves wholeheartedly to the desegregation of the public schools they would find the physical task of redistributing the school population much easier than would the officials of many northern school districts. If they would accept the idea of "busing" children to achieve racial balance, as they have long required the transportation of black children to preserve segregation, they would not have to bus so many children so far as would New York City. By the same token, the belated but continuing expansion of industry in the South creates opportunities for establishing new patterns of employment without raising the specter of "laying off white workers to make jobs for blacks."

To the extent that blacks choose to utilize parallel institutions (for example, black businesses and "community-controlled schools") as a steppingstone toward acceptance, they may have an advantage in the South. Despite handicaps, significant black economic development has taken place within the framework of segregation. The largest black-owned insurance company in the United States has its headquarters in Durham, North Carolina. Atlanta boasts a strong black-owned bank. Although the South lags slightly behind the nation in the ratio of self-employed male businessmen who are black and although the feasibility of a separate economy is doubtful, there is an existing base for the development of black business in the region.[19] In education there is an even broader base for the improvement of black-controlled institutions. Although they are undeniably inferior, the great majority of black colleges and universities are in the South. Some have proud traditions of excellence in music, athletics, and community leadership; they are challenged now to take a leading role in developing new techniques for teaching the educationally disadvantaged student. If southerners, both white and black, can come to regard black institutions as continuing to exist because black people want them rather than being the inferior product of unwanted rejection, then a new basis for white respect and black pride might emerge.

The development of this new respect depends on a dramatic change in the attitude of many white southerners. John Egerton has observed:

> The notion that the South, where Negroes were systematically dehumanized and where white supremacy still has not surrendered its hold, could somehow be the place where equality and justice will first be attained in this country is a laughable absurdity to most nonsoutherners—and probably to a majority of southerners as well.[20]

Egerton cites James McBride Dabbs, of "Rips Raps Plantation," South Carolina, former president of the Southern Regional Council, as an exemplar of southerners who "share the belief that the key to racial reconciliation in America—if there is one—will be found in the South." Dabbs holds to a firm belief that kindness is as much a part of the essence of the southern heritage as is white supremacy. He said to Egerton in an interview:

> The system has been wrong and unjust, but somehow there have been virtues—many small, perhaps, maybe some great—woven into the system. The southern emphasis on decency, kindness, manners and so on was built partly because the southerner didn't have the courage and imagination to wipe out the injustice, so he just did what he could to make it a little more human.[21]

C. Vann Woodward has developed the theme that the distinctiveness of the South rests in its inability to accept with full confidence the national legend of success, victory, and prosperity.[22] Dabbs believes that the white southern history of defeat binds whites and blacks and challenges them alike:

> Challenges us all, whites and Negroes together. For we are together in the South. The tragic view of our history —and of its core, the Civil War—shows how close together. Each race has suffered because of the other's presence, but each has found some wisdom. The basic wisdom we have acquired is the wisdom of those whose lives have been entwined in suffering and defeat. I don't think it makes much difference what causes the suffering, who causes the defeat. We have been together in it; and we have learned, at our best, a certain tolerance, a certain gentleness, a certain understanding.[23]

Leslie Dunbar, another white southern liberal, suggests that the peculiarly southern sense of community and the common experience of poverty constitute a binding tie betwen white and black southerners. Contending that "the general conformity of the liberal to social practices which he opposes is a mark of his dogged refusal to alienate himself from southern society," he continues:

> On the whole, this attitude of respect toward the community is not alien to a great many of the Negro leaders.

And on the whole, this shared attitude presents the only real possibility, for those of us who want one, of preserving the South as a cultural organism, and not merely as a cultivated, but mummified, memory, analogous to New England. It is not a very strong possibility, though the relative poverty of the region may help along its chances: poverty is a strong folk-tie.[24]

Frank P. Graham, North Carolina's great but persecuted liberal son, has described the South as a place where a new, benevolent pattern of race relations may develop:

> In the old South, where human slavery made one of its last stands in the modern world, industrialism has made fresh beginnings on productive soil. The people of the South have the tragic lessons of one and the opportunities of the other to build a fairer civilization than the races in the South or industrialism in the world have seen. In a pleasant land under a southern sun between the Chesapeake and the Gulf, a friendly folk will, we trust, work out together our integration.[25]

Even some of the radical youth of the New Left have taken up this theme. Prior to its dissolution in 1969 as a result of a conflict with the predominantly nonsouthern Students for a Democratic Society, the Southern Student Organizing Committee issued a plea for "southern consciousness." An Atlanta journalist said of this appeal:

> This kind of "Southern consciousness" is narrow and ideological, limited by a class-warfare view of the world. But there is more to SSOC's perception of the South. It sees that the South has a heritage of personalism within a folk culture (black and white), placing high value on man-to-man relations on the very personal level. And it sees that the growth of cities and industrialism threaten this heritage, much of which had its origins in Southerners' closeness to the land and the frontier.[26]

The possibility that the South may show the nation the way to racial harmony cannot be dismissed lightly, for it is a land of paradoxes and surprises. For example, following a year when New York City and its liberal mayor, John Lindsay, had been caught in the throes of a school conflict largely involving blacks and Jews, the city of Atlanta astounded the nation with a sudden display of interracial harmony. A coalition of blacks and white liberals garnered enough votes to elect a Jewish mayor and a black vice-mayor in November 1969, at the same time that Lindsay won reelection only as an independent candidate with less than a majority of the vote.

Social scientists have not yet devised instruments to test Dabb's assertion that "there's more human nature in the South than anywhere else in this country." Certainly there are many white southerners, most of them with beliefs that are far removed from the liberalism of Dabbs, Graham, Woodward, and McGill, who cling to the folk-belief that southerners are indeed a" friendly folk." Before social scientists get around to reducing this belief to an hypothesis, it may be put to a crucial test by the demands of militant blacks for a new South and a new America.

THE WAY OF WHITE SUPREMACY. The other course that white southerners might follow would also lead to a new America, but not the one desired by black Americans. Liberalism, besieged from both Right and Left, is in retreat not only in the South but all over the nation. In 1968 the southern states, save the five that gave their votes to George Wallace, were a crucial part of a coalition that returned a Republican to the White House. By 1969 there was evidence that the confidence of black Americans in the federal government, already waning under the administration of Lyndon B. Johnson, had reached a new low. A *Newsweek* opinion poll in 1963 had showed that, under the Kennedy administration, 88 percent of blacks thought that the federal government was helpful to Negro rights. By 1966 the proportion had declined to 74 percent. In 1969, only 25 percent of blacks saw the federal government as helpful.[27]

While optimistic, liberal white southerners may argue for the reality of a humane tradition in the South, they cannot deny or wish away the heritage of white supremacy. It is not that white southerners have been the only racists in the country; this myth has been dispelled by black critics to an extent that southern apologists were never able to accomplish. While white Americans in other regions practiced racism, however, only white southerners made of it an ideology. The South is still the only region in which open espousal of this ideology is a political asset, although some cities (Los Angeles, for example) are becoming more "southern" in this respect. At the same time, the South lacks a strong tradition of liberalism, or radicalism. The labor movement had its major development outside the South and, although its maturity has been characterized by increasing conservatism, it is still relatively weak in the region.

Ever since the advent of the slavery controversy over a century ago, the plaintive cry of white southerners as a conscious minority has been, "The majority is helping black men at insufferable cost to us." During the recent years of the black revolution, however, this cry has begun to be taken up by a multitude of whites all over the land. Peter Schrag, calling this type of white man "the forgotten American," describes him:

> There is hardly a language to describe him, or even a set of social statistics. Just names: racist-bigot-redneck-ethnic-Irish-Italian-Pole-Hunkie-Yahoo. The lower middle class. A blank. . . . Who watches the tube, plays the horses, and keeps niggers out of his union and his neighborhood. Who might vote for Wallace (but didn't). . . . Who is free, white, and twenty-one, has a job, a home, a family, and is up to his eyeballs in credit. . . . He was once the hero of the civics books, the man that Andrew Jackson called "the bone and sinew of the country." Now he is "the forgotten man," perhaps the most alienated person in America.[28]

A University of Michigan survey conducted in 1968 in fifteen cities showed that a majority of whites did not accept the contention that discrimination against blacks was the nation's number one problem:

> The whites were asked whether Negroes with the same level of education as their own were relatively better or

worse off than they. Forty-two per cent said better off
and 46 per cent about the same; only 5 per cent said
worse. The interviewers then cited figures showing that
Negroes had worse jobs, education, and housing, and
asked why the white respondents thought that was so.
Nineteen per cent said it was because of discrimination,
56 per cent said it was "mainly due to something about
the Negroes themselves," and 19 per cent thought it was
a mixture of both.[29]

The Urban Coalition and Urban America, Inc., assessing the
response to the report of the National Advisory Commission
on Civil Disorders one year after the report was issued concluded that there was rising discontent among millions of
white Americans not only over the national emphasis on the
problems of blacks but also about their own grievances—
rising prices, rising taxes, changing morals, and public
order.[30] The incessant urgency of the black protest, the violence suggested by its rhetoric, the actual increase in crime
and disorder, the myths created by mass media that exaggerate
this increase, the wave of campus revolts, all combined to project an image of mounting chaos that the government was
unable or unwilling to combat.

It has happened before in history that a citizenry that feels
its property and lives threatened by disorder has demanded
of the state an increase of social control, even at the expense
of the freedom of its own members. Irving Horowitz and
Martin Liebowitz have analyzed the consequences of this folk
response in terms of political theory:

   The solution to the problem of chaos or the *Anarch* is
the *Leviathan*. But the *Leviathan* is the *totalitarian* State.
Indeed, totalitarianism is the perfect solution to the
problem of disorder. The dilemma for those who consider social problems obstacles to be overcome is that
any true overcoming of social problems implies a perfect
social system. And this entails several goals: first, the
total institutionalization of all people; second, the
thoroughgoing equilibrium between the parts of a system
with respect to their functioning and the functioning of

other sectors; third, the elimination of social change as either a fact or value. Thus, the resolution of social problems from the point of view of the social system would signify the totalitarian resolution of social life.[31]

To achieve this sort of resolution fearful people have always looked for a "strong man" who would restore order. They seek a dictator in the ancient Roman sense, a hero who will combat the enemies of law and order and protect the law-abiding common man. That he may become the arbitrary ruler and oppressor of all is never contemplated in the beginning.

If the forgotten Americans seek such a strong man, he may not be a white southerner but this minority will be crucial to his success. There are reactionary elements in every region who can provide likely candidates for the role—some have already attained high municipal or state offices. White southerners can see that black Americans as a group are more and more coming to be regarded as the chief agent of disorder. George Wallace staked his bid for national power on the intuition that "as the Second Reconstruction amplified over the rest of the nation and became a national crisis, there would be the same kind of backfire in white communities—'then you gonna see the common folks all over the rest of this country Southernized.'" Convinced of the accuracy of his prediction, the Alabaman tried to evangelize the rest of the nation with that part of the white southern gospel symbolized by white supremacy, the closed society, and the tough county sheriff. It is true, as Schrag pointed out, that the "forgotten American" outside the South failed to vote for Wallace at the last minute, despite the indications of preelection polls. But Marshall Frady, Wallace's unsympathetic biographer, identified the profound significance of his candidacy:

> In an almost mystical way, he answered the vague sense of dread and inadequacy among those uncounted submerged souls in America leading what are mostly lives of quiet scrabbling desperation—who now, through the immediacy of television, feel menaced by confrontations and figures remote from their existence, which in another time would have remained quite abstract to them.

This was the unsuspected constituency disclosed by Wallace's candidacy. His campaign acted as a litmus for this reality about the nation at this time and it may be that this discovery will be his real and lasting importance.[32]

Wallace may not be the strong man who may some day successfully exploit this constituency. Whoever does so will certainly look to the white South as a firm base of support, however. The victories of Barry Goldwater and George Wallace in five states of the Deep South in their unsuccessful campaigns, and Richard Nixon's sweep of the rest of the South in 1968, provide evidence of the region's enduring conservatism. (See Appendix, Chart 2.) The emergence of President Nixon's "southern strategy" after his election could serve only to encourage this conservatism.

Southerners are a heterogeneous lot. There are black southerners, white liberals, Catholics, Jews, and transplanted Yankees. Both national and local elections since the Johnson landslide of 1964 suggest, however, that the majority of white southerners cling to the belief that the United States is and should be a white man's society. They have new cause for hope that, instead of hypocritically castigating them, the rest of the nation will now join, even follow, them:

> They see national support for the Negro's cause melting away. The diehard white Southerner's politicians reason that they can run on a platform of defiance and retrogression and win. The white reactionary voter . . . believes that he can elect politicians who preach defiance with, at last, some expectation of seing the defiance succeed.
>
> All this the white segregationist voter has concluded from the events of recent months. He is convinced that things now are shifting in his favor. He sees the time coming when he no longer will have to accommodate national pressures to provide justice to his Negro neighbors. At last the southern segregationist sees evidence to warrant his long-cherished belief that the white North shares his prejudices.[33]

A Minority No More?

Throughout most of their history white southerners have believed that they were a minority and have acted as if they were. Intensely conscious of the dilemma of minority rights versus majority rule, they pioneered in the exploration of sources of minority protection. Liberal and conservative alike, white southern spokesman have protested against their region's role as the scapegoat for the nation's sins of racism. Clinging to their regional identity, even defying the authority of the federal government, they have continued to assert the fundamental purity of their Americanism. By openly denying the national myth that American democracy is color-blind, they have instigated civil war and civil disorders. The fire-eating reactionaries among white southerners time and again have brought the wrath of the rest of the nation and the armies of the federal government down upon the homeland because they have refused to pay even lip service to the idea that in America all men are equal. Yet, as Howard Zinn, a white southerner who fought segregation as a member of SNCC, has argued:

> The South, far from being utterly different, is really the *essence* of the nation. . . . Those very qualities long attributed to the South as special possessions are, in truth, *American* qualities, and the nation reacts emotionally to the South precisely because it subconsciously recognizes itself there.[34]

Now white southerners find another minority, a group that has been their ancient problem, cast in the role of dissenter from the national myths and disturber of the peace. The challenge to majority rule comes from blacks, not from white southerners. The thinly veiled racism of white Americans in other regions has been exposed, and the wrath of the nation has turned from the white southern minority to the black minority. If this national trend toward angry white reaction to black desperation continues, white southerners, except for the forlorn liberals, may find a short cut to their own integration into the larger American society. They may cease to be a minority in an America in which white supremacy is an ideal as well as a fact.

The Significance of a Quasi-Minority

White southerners constitute the most mariginal type of minority in the United States. They might well be called a quasi-minority, for the evidence of their minority-like subjective reaction to their status is much stronger than the evidence that they are badly mistreated. They have encountered no color bar. Their cultural differences have been slight, consisting of regional variations of Old American culture, not of foreign traits imported by recent immigrants. The differences in values that have at times set them at odds with other Americans arise from their exaggeration of values shared by many other Americans, such as white supremacy and Protestant Christianity.

Even white southern spokesmen disagree on the validity of the charge that the South, as a region, has been the victim of economic discrimination. Although there is certainly some discrimination against the "hillbillies" outside the South, they do not encounter such formidable barriers to individual social mobility as do blacks, Mexican Americans and Puerto Ricans in the same cities. As a minority, white southerners have not suffered the degree of differential and unequal treatment to which most minorities have to adjust.

They have, nevertheless, reacted as a defensive, self-conscious minority, regarding themselves as the object of collective discrimination. As a limiting case of a minority group, reacting to discrimination even though it is minimal, the white southerners underscore certain aspects of minority group relations that are often neglected.

In a paradoxical fashion they provide support for Pierre van den Berghe's admonition that "race must be clearly recognized as a *subjective* and *social* reality."[35] Nowhere in the literature of race relations will there be found a theory that the problems of white southerners as a class have arisen from their biologi-

cal inferiority. True, Mencken revived an old, ante-bellum
theory that southern poor whites represented a biologically
inferior stock. Some hillbillies were found to refer to white
southerners as a race, but with connotations of superiority, not
inferiority. The "scientific racists" of the late nineteenth and
twentieth centuries, obsessed with the notion of Caucasian
superiority and sometimes with the special virtues of north
European ancestry, have never seen fit to classify white southerners as one of the inferior races.

It is interesting to note that, ever since the armed services
started using mental tests to screen inductees in World War I,
whites from the South, as a group, have scored lower than
whites from other regions. During World War II the rate of
rejection of white males on mental or educational grounds
was 51 per 1,000 for the Southeast, but only 22 per 1,000
nationally.[36] Between 1958 and 1966 the percentage of whites
from the census South failing the Armed Forces Qualification
Test was 11.0, compared with 7.2 percent for the nation.[37]

In the light of the abundant evidence that mental or intelligence test results reflect educational experience as well as
innate capacity, no case for the biological inferiority of white
southerners should be inferred from these figures. Yet it is the
consistently high rates of failure of black subjects on these
same tests that such critics as Henry Garrett, Francis McGurk,
and Audrey M. Shuey have used in denouncing the "radical
environmentalism" of scientists who question the existence of
racial differences in intelligence.[38] Scientists and laymen who
argue that the existence of racial differences in intelligence
should be assumed until positively disproven seem to experience no difficulty, however, in swallowing an environmentalist
explanation of white southern deficiencies in test intelligence.
It may be postulated that popular notions of races and a racial
hierarchy have had greater influence on scientific concepts
than vice versa.

Even though some of them think of themselves and their
kind as a race, the so-called hillbillies clearly constitute an
ethnic group in northern cities. Their experience underscores
the fact that only a minimal degree of cultural differentiation

is needed for a group to be recognized, invidiously stereotyped, and treated in a categorical fashion. But categorization is a product of both visibility and density. If great symbolic importance is attached, because of historical factors, to a trait that gives members of a group visibility, then even a few representatives may encounter discrimination at the hands of a larger, dominant group. On the other hand, high density of minority group members may lead to an increase of prejudice and discrimination despite the low salience of the differentiating traits.

Finally, the case of the white southerners indicates that the perceptions of the minority group must be regarded as an essential variable that interacts with the behavior of the dominant group in determining the course of intergroup relations. Sympathy for oppressed minorities, stemming from a liberal and democratic ethos, suggests that when a victimized people cries "discrimination," the discrimination is proportionate to the strength of the cry. Throughout their history, however, white southerners have been given to exaggerating the degree of discrimination against them and to minimizing the extent of their own discrimination against black southerners. There are no doubt some observers who would contend that the white southerners' complaints of discrimination are totally unfounded. Yet it has been shown that the group has time and time again acted as if it were indeed a persecuted minority.

This is merely another illustration of the validity of W. I. Thomas' dictum that "if men define situations as real, they are real in their consequences." The consequences of a minority's magnification of the extent of discrimination against it are just as real when the actual discrimination is great as when it is minor, as it is in the case of white southerners. The reaction of the minority to discrimination, both real and imagined, may evoke increased hostility from the dominant group and lead to an intensification of conflict. This has been the experience of white southerners. Although the study of the prejudice and discrimination of dominant groups is essential to the understanding of racial and ethnic relations, so also is the analysis of the defensive reactions of minority groups.

Notes

1 C. Vann Woodward, *The Burden of Southern History* (Baton Rouge: Louisiana State University Press, 1968), p. 25.

2 Pierre L. van den Berghe, *Race and Racism* (New York: Wiley, 1967), p. 18.

3 *Ibid.*, p. 77.

4 C. Vann Woodward, "From the First Reconstruction to the Second," in Willie Morris (ed.), *The South Today* (New York: Harper & Row, 1965), p. 14.

5 Milton M. Gordon, *Assimilation in American Life* (New York: Oxford University Press, 1964), p. 24.

6 *Ibid.*, pp. 234–235.

7 Jesse T. Carpenter, *The South as a Conscious Minority* (New York: New York University Press, 1930), p. 4.

8 "Interposition vs. Judicial Power," *Race Relations Law Reporter*, 1 (April 1956), 470.

9 "Report from Black America," *Newsweek*, June 30, 1969, p. 19.

10 Stokely Carmichael and Charles V. Hamilton, *Black Power* (New York: Vintage, 1967), p. 166.

11 Francis B. Simkins, *A History of the South* (New York: Knopf, 1963), p. 113.

12 Jack Newfield, *A Prophetic Minority* (New York: Signet, 1966), p. 91.

13 Charles V. Hamilton, "Riots, Revolts and Relevant Response," in Floyd B. Barbour (ed.), *The Black Power Revolt* (Boston: Porter Sargent, 1968), pp. 176–177.

14 Newfield, *op. cit.*, pp. 72–73.

15 Hamilton, "Riots, Revolts and Relevant Response," *op. cit.*, pp. 174–175.

16 Robert S. Browne, "A Case for Separatism," in *Separatism or Integration: Which Way for America?* (New York: A. Philip Randolph Education Fund, 1968), p. 13.

17 Bayard Rustin, "Toward Integration as a Goal," in *Separatism or Integration: Which Way for America? op. cit*, p. 20.

18 Woodward, *The Burden of Southern History, op. cit.*, p. 10.

19 See Leonard Broom and Norval Glenn, *The Transformation of the Negro American* (New York: Harper & Row, 1965), pp. 136–143.

[20] John Egerton, "A Visit with James McBride Dabbs," *New South*, 24 (Winter 1969), 41.

[21] *Ibid.*, p. 44.

[22] Woodward, *The Burden of Southern History, op. cit.*, chap. 9.

[23] James McBride Dabbs, in *A Hundred Years Later* (Atlanta: Southern Regional Council, 1962), p. 7.

[24] Leslie W. Dunbar, "The Changing Mind of the South: The Exposed Nerve," *The Journal of Politics*, 26 (February 1964), 7–8.

[25] Frank P. Graham, in *A Hundred Years Later, op. cit.*, p. 26.

[26] Reese Cleghorn, "Southern Consciousness," *South Today*, 1 (August 1969), 1.

[27] William Brink and Louis Harris, *The Negro Revolution in America* (New York: Simon and Schuster, 1964), p. 131, and *Newsweek*, June 30, 1969, p. 19.

[28] Peter Schrag, "The Forgotten American," *Harper's*, August 1969, p. 27.

[29] Urban America, Inc. and the Urban Coalition, *One Year Later* (New York: Praeger, 1969), pp. 103–104.

[30] *Ibid.*, p. 106.

[31] Irving L. Horowitz and Martin Liebowitz, "Social Deviance and Political Marginality: Toward a Redefinition of the Relations between Sociology and Politics," *Social Problems*, 15 (Winter 1968), 295.

[32] Marshall Frady, "Gary, Indiana," *Harper's*, August 1969, p. 37.

[33] John H. Wheeler, "Of Conflict, Growth and Future Progress," *New South*, 22 (Winter 1967), 3.

[34] Howard Zinn, *The Southern Mystique* (New York: Knopf, 1964), p. 218.

[35] Van den Berghe, *op. cit.*, p. 148.

[36] Eli Ginzberg, *The Lost Divisions* (New York: Columbia University Press, 1959), table 38, pp. 156–157.

[37] Bernard D. Karpinos, "Mental Test Failures," in Sol Tax (ed.), *The Draft* (Chicago: University of Chicago Press, 1967), pp. 46–48.

[38] See Audrey M. Shuey, *The Testing of Negro Intelligence* (Lynchburg, Va.: Bell, 1958).

⊚ Selected
Bibliography

Arnall, Ellis G. *The Shore Dimly Seen*. Philadelphia: Lippincott, 1946.
A political analysis by a former governor of Georgia of the South's role in the New Deal. Contains an explicit development of the theme that the South is a minority region.

Brandfon, Robert L. *The American South in the Twentieth Century*. New York: Crowell, 1967.
A collection of original documents revealing the positions of various types of southerners on such topics as civil rights for blacks, organized labor, politics, and agriculture, from 1900 through 1965. Contains a statement of the doctrine of interposition made in 1955 by a Virginia legislative committee.

Cash, W. J. *The Mind of the South*. New York: Knopf, 1941.
Written in 1940 but still timely. Argues that the South is different from other regions. Attacks the myth of the Old South of cavaliers and their ladies as well as the myth of a New South that has made a complete break with tradition.

Dabbs, James M. *The Southern Heritage*. New York: Knopf, 1958.
A hopeful, loving statement of the humanity in the southern heritage. Written by a liberal white southerner who fights for the civil rights of black southerners from his ancestral home on a plantation in South Carolina.

Dabney, Virginius. *Below the Potomac*. New York: Appleton-Century, 1942.
One of the liberal southern editors of the Roosevelt era analyzes the progress the South has made toward "catching up" with the rest of the nation. A companion piece

to books by Jonathan Daniels, Ellis Arnall, and Ralph McGill.

Daniels, Jonathan. *A Southerner Discovers the South.* New York: MacMillan, 1938.
One of several books in which liberal southern newspaper editors assessed the condition of the region toward the end of the Depression and predicted the emergence of a New South. Reflects both the regional pride and the minority defensiveness of the loyal but critical white southerner.

Franklin, John Hope. *The Militant South.* Cambridge: Harvard University Press, 1956.
A black historian argues that violence has always been an important feature of the culture of the South and that the tradition of a military spirit helped to pave the way for secession and civil war.

Grantham, Dewey W., Jr., (ed.). *The South and the Sectional Image.* New York: Harper & Row, 1967.
Essays by southern sociologists, economists, political scientists, and historians on the various aspects of "southernism." Includes a discussion of southern mythology and a critique of the theme that the South is a colonial region.

Greenhut, Melvin L., and W. Tate Whitman (eds.). *Essays in Southern Economic Development.* Chapel Hill: University of North Carolina Press, 1964.
An up-to-date analysis of the economic problems of the South and the region's place in the national economy. Includes analyses of the effects of differential freight rates and municipal subsidies to new industry on southern economic development.

Journal of Social Issues, Vol. 22, January 1966.
A special issue devoted to urbanization and social change in the South.

Killian, Lewis M. "The Adjustment of Southern White Workers to Northern, Urban Norms." *Social Forces,* Vol. 32 (October 1953).
Analyzes the position of white, southern, working-class

migrants in Chicago, showing that they perceive themselves as a minority group powerless to challenge northern norms that violate the racial etiquette of the South.

Lerche, Charles O. *The Uncertain South*. Chicago: Quadrangle,
1964.
An examination of the political effects of the urbanization of the South as reflected in the voting of southern
congressmen on foreign affairs.

Matthews, Donald R., and James W. Prothro. *Negroes and the
New Southern Politics*. New York: Harcourt, Brace &
World, 1966.
Examines the present and potential roles of black south-
erners in the region as a whole and in various types of
southern communities.

McGill, Ralph. *The South and the Southerner*. Boston: Little,
Brown, 1964.
Partly autobiographical analysis of what it means to be
a white southerner by a famous southern liberal. Portrays
poignantly the complexity of the relations between various
types of southerners.

McKinney, John C., and Edgar T. Thompson, (eds.). *The
South in Continuity and Change*. Durham, N.C.: Duke
University Press, 1965.
Essays by sociologists, most of them southerners, on
various aspects of southern life as the region moves
toward industrialization and urbanization.

Morris, Willie. *North Toward Home*. Boston: Houghton Mifflin,
1967.
The autobiography of a white southern expatriate, cover-
ing the period from his childhood in a Mississippi town
to his acceptance of New York City as home. Reveals the
ambivalence the liberal white southerner feels toward
the South and his feeling of being an outsider when he
leaves the region.

Morris, Willie, (ed.). *The South Today*. New York: Harper &
Row, 1965.
Essays on the South during the civil rights crisis, mostly
by southern writers, white and black, conservative and
liberal.

Nicholls, William H. *Southern Tradition and Regional Progress*. Chapel Hill: University of North Carolina Press, 1960.
A critical examination of changes in the twentieth-century South and of barriers to its progress.

Odum, Howard W. *Southern Regions of the United States*. Chapel Hill: University of North Carolina Press, 1936.
The classic attempt to define the South as a region on the basis of sociocultural indices. Although many of the statistics are out of date, this volume constitutes a comprehensive analysis of the nature of the South and its people during a critical period in history, the Great Depression.

Phillips, Kevin P. *The Emerging Republican Majority*. New Rochelle, N.Y.: Arlington House, 1969.
One of President Richard Nixon's campaign managers in the 1968 election argues that white southerners will be part of a New Republican coalition that will strip the Democratic "Liberal Establishment" of its power and introduce a new era in American politics.

Potter, David M. *The South and the Sectional Conflict*. Baton Rouge: Louisiana State University Press, 1968.
Recommended especially for the first section, which explores the enigmatic relationship between "southernism" and nationalism.

Powdermaker, Hortense. *After Freedom*. New York: Atheneum, 1968.
One of the best studies of the social structure of a town in the Deep South in the 1930s, recently reissued as a paperback. Focuses on the black community, but contains an excellent description of social class in the white community.

Ransom, John C., *et. al.*, (eds.). *I'll Take My Stand*. New York: Harper and Brothers, 1930.
The controversial statement by twelve southern authors of the so-called Agrarian school, extolling the virtues of southern agrarianism and warning against the deleterious effects that urbanization and industrialization would have on southern culture.

Rubin, Louis D., Jr., and James J. Kilpatrick (eds.). *The Lasting South*. Chicago: Regnery, 1957.
A collection of essays on the South at the beginning of the civil rights crisis, most of them written from a conservative southern viewpoint. Includes modern defenses of what the contributors regard as the virtues of the Confederacy.

Silver, James W. *Mississippi: The Closed Society*. New York: Harcourt, Brace & World, 1963.
Based on the author's experiences and observations at the University of Mississippi when the desegregation controversy was at its height, shows the repressive effects of southern racial orthodoxy.

Woodward, C. Vann. *The Burden of Southern History*. Baton Rouge: Louisiana State University Press, 1968.
A collection of essays by one of the leading historians of the South dealing with such topics as southern identity, southern writers, Populism, the civil rights movement, and the relevance of the southern heritage to American nationalism.

◎ Appendix

Chart 1
States of the South, with Dates of Statehood

Chart 2
Presidential Preference in Terms of Electoral Votes,
Southern States, 1948–1968

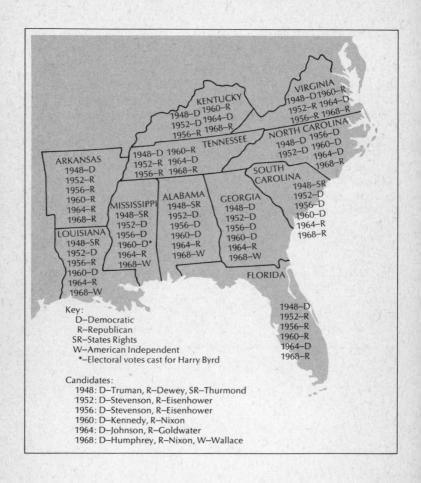

Key:
  D—Democratic
  R—Republican
  SR—States Rights
  W—American Independent
  *—Electoral votes cast for Harry Byrd

Candidates:
  1948: D—Truman, R—Dewey, SR—Thurmond
  1952: D—Stevenson, R—Eisenhower
  1956: D—Stevenson, R—Eisenhower
  1960: D—Kennedy, R—Nixon
  1964: D—Johnson, R—Goldwater
  1968: D—Humphrey, R—Nixon, W—Wallace

Table 1

Population of the South, White and Black, 1790–1960*

YEAR	WHITE	BLACK	ALL†	% WHITE
1790	1,016,430	565,919	1,582,349	64.2
1800	1,427,321	774,666	2,201,987	64.8
1810	1,885,017	1,097,813	2,982,884	63.2
1820	2,437,451	1,447,653	3,885,104	62.7
1830	3,169,691	1,974,535	5,144,226	61.6
1840	3,881,330	2,638,583	6,519,913	59.5
1850	4,949,327	3,904,440	8,043,767	61.5
1860	5,945,812	3,707,116	9,654,801	61.6
1870	6,080,480	3,907,740	9,989,818	60.9
1880	7,802,194	5,238,365	13,047,187	59.8
1890	9,423,633	5,878,492	15,329,806	61.5
1900	11,211,931	6,850,601	18,074,129	62.0
1910	13,271,355	7,499,716	20,785,777	63.8
1920	15,291,408	7,550,004	22,860,356	66.9
1930	17,745,903	7,778,473	25,550,898	69.5
1940	20,059,368	8,168,552	28,261,829	71.0
1950	23,455,719	8,277,206	31,785,887	73.8
1960	27,920,263	8,891,185	36,893,794	75.7

* "The South" defined as Virginia, North Carolina, South Carolina, Georgia, Florida, Kentucky, Tennessee, Alabama, Mississippi, Arkansas, and Louisiana.

† Includes other races after 1860.

SOURCE: Statistical Abstracts of the United States.

Table 2

Net Gain or Loss of Native White Population by Interstate
Movement for Southern States, 1920–1960

STATE	1920	1930	1940	1950	1960
Virginia	−193,348	−244,088	−129,037	+80,410	+174,828
North Carolina	−172,291	−129,036	−119,681	−170,694	−253,268
South Carolina	−43,002	−69,292	−50,039	−56,300	−35,576
Georgia	−132,563	−249,280	−223,352	−230,535	−194,890
Florida	+194,666	+397,059	+563,928	+948,075	+2,021,282
Kentucky	−479,584	−603,884	−597,051	−793,175	−1,015,415
Tennessee	−362,589	−393,727	−346,382	−343,085	−488,922
Alabama	−147,514	−192,246	−264,308	−336,705	−440,633
Mississippi	−169,448	−183,446	−188,740	−263,605	−338,966
Arkansas	−16,920	−208,581	−326,783	−537,650	−749,383
Louisiana	+15,753	−8,784	+7,463	−9,945	+8,522
The South	−1,506,840	−1,885,305	−1,683,982	−1,713,209	−1,312,421

SOURCE: U.S. Census of Population, 1920, 1930, 1940, 1950, 1960.

Table 3

Parentage of Native Whites,
The South and the United States, 1910–1960*
The South

YEAR	NATIVE WHITE PARENT- AGE	FOREIGN OR MIXED PARENT- AGE	TOTAL NATIVE WHITES	% Native Whites of Native Parentage	
				SOUTH	U.S.
1910	12,554,539	483,730	13,038,269	96.3	72.4
1920	14,535,305	521,839	15,057,144	96.5	72.0
1930	16,970,456	559,706	17,530,162	96.8	73.1
1940	18,817,820	457,820	19,275,640	97.6	78.4
1950	22,466,755	646,705	23,113,460	97.2	81.0
1960	26,496,485	972,948	27,469,433	96.5	84.1

* Foreign-born whites have constituted a negligible proportion of the population of the South since 1900 and are, therefore, excluded from this measure of the "Americanness" of white southerners.

SOURCE: U.S. Census of Population, 1910, 1920, 1930, 1940, 1950, 1960.

Table 4

Rank of Southern States According to Percent
of Population Classified as Urban,
1910 and 1960

	Rank		Percent Urban	
STATE	1910	1960	1910	1960
Virginia	36	33	23.1	55.6
North Carolina	45	45	14.4	39.5
South Carolina	44	44	14.8	41.2
Georgia	38	34	20.6	55.3
Florida	31	13	29.1	73.9
Kentucky	34	42	24.3	44.5
Tennessee	39	38	20.2	52.3
Alabama	42	35	17.3	54.8
Mississippi	49	50	11.5	37.7
Arkansas	48	43	12.9	42.8
Louisiana	28	25	30.0	63.3
The South			19.8	51.0
United States			45.7	69.9

SOURCE: U.S. Census of Population: 1960.
Subject Reports, *Number of Inhabitants*,
PC(1)-1A, Table G, p. XVII and Table 20,
p. 29.

Table 5

Percent of Southern Population Classified as Urban,

By States, 1790–1960

	VA.	N.C.	S.C.	GA.	FLA.	KY.	TENN.	ALA.	MISS.	ARK.	LA.	SOUTH	U.S.
1790	1.8	0.0	6.6	0.0	*	0.0	0.0	*	*	*	*	1.4	5.1
1800	2.6	0.0	5.4	3.2	*	0.0	0.0	0.0	0.0	*	*	1.4	6.1
1810	3.6	0.0	6.0	2.1	*	1.1	0.0	0.0	0.0	0.0	22.5	3.5	7.3
1820	3.8	2.0	4.9	2.2	*	1.6	0.0	0.0	0.0	0.0	17.7	3.2	7.2
1830	4.8	1.4	5.8	2.7	0.0	2.4	.8	1.0	0.0	0.0	21.4	3.8	8.8
1840	6.9	1.8	5.7	3.6	0.0	4.0	.8	2.1	1.0	0.0	29.9	5.1	10.8
1850	8.0	2.4	7.3	4.3	0.0	7.5	2.2	4.6	1.8	0.0	26.0	5.8	15.3
1860	9.5	2.5	6.9	7.1	4.1	10.4	4.2	5.1	2.6	.9	26.1	7.2	19.8
1870	11.9	3.4	8.6	8.4	8.1	14.8	7.5	6.3	4.0	2.6	27.9	9.4	25.7
1880	12.5	3.9	7.5	9.4	10.0	15.2	7.5	5.4	3.1	4.0	25.5	9.5	28.2
1890	17.1	7.2	10.1	14.0	19.8	19.2	13.5	10.1	5.4	6.5	25.4	13.5	35.1
1900	18.3	9.9	12.8	15.6	20.3	21.8	16.2	11.9	7.7	8.5	26.5	15.4	39.7
1910	23.1	14.4	14.8	20.6	29.1	24.3	20.2	17.3	11.5	12.9	30.0	19.8	45.7
1920	29.2	19.2	17.5	25.1	36.5	26.2	26.1	21.7	13.4	16.6	34.9	24.2	51.2
1930	32.4	25.5	21.3	30.8	51.7	30.6	34.3	28.1	16.9	20.6	39.7	30.2	56.2
1940	25.3	27.3	24.5	34.4	55.1	29.8	35.2	30.2	19.8	22.6	41.5	32.3	56.5
1950	47.0	33.7	36.7	45.3	65.5	36.8	44.1	43.8	27.9	33.0	54.8	42.6	64.0
1960	55.6	39.5	41.2	55.3	73.9	44.5	52.3	54.8	37.7	42.8	63.3	51.0	69.9

* Not enumerated.

SOURCE: U.S. Census of Population: 1960. Subject Reports, *Number of Inhabitants*, PC(1)-1A, Table 20, p. 34.

Table 6

White Population Born in Other Divisions by State of Residence in the South, 1960

Division of Birth

STATE OF RESIDENCE, 1960	NEW ENGLAND	MIDDLE ATLANTIC	EAST NORTH CENTRAL	WEST NORTH CENTRAL	MOUNTAIN	PACIFIC	TOTAL
Virginia	49,733	165,323	97,391	51,639	14,694	31,962	410,742
North Carolina	20,554	60,752	44,111	18,971	6,056	12,375	162,819
South Carolina	11,810	30,478	22,488	10,643	3,447	7,491	86,357
Georgia	16,599	50,256	53,588	25,158	7,531	13,729	166,861
Florida	169,992	563,747	487,506	118,766	19,668	37,093	1,396,722
Kentucky	7,205	31,038	140,032	21,561	4,754	7,216	211,806
Tennessee	8,755	26,763	69,383	33,524	6,183	11,535	156,143
Alabama	7,209	22,680	38,444	18,737	5,334	8,612	101,016
Mississippi	4,281	10,417	21,210	13,687	3,824	6,086	59,505
Arkansas	2,472	7,973	38,697	66,764	8,048	14,092	138,046
Louisiana	7,327	23,477	34,862	29,502	8,080	12,179	115,427
The South	305,937	992,904	1,047,712	408,952	87,619	162,370	3,005,494
Percent of White Population of the South	1.1	3.6	3.8	1.5	.3	.6	10.8

SOURCE: U.S. Census of Population: 1960. Subject Reports, *State of Birth*, (PC(2)-2A, Table 18 and 19.

Table 7

Native Whites Born in the South Living in Other Divisions of the U.S., 1960

Division of Residence, 1960

STATE OF BIRTH	NEW ENGLAND	MIDDLE ATLANTIC	EAST NORTH CENTRAL	WEST NORTH CENTRAL	MOUNTAIN	PACIFIC
Virginia	21,345	87,866	113,602	19,998	17,806	66,823
North Carolina	15,427	57,039	60,962	14,732	16,528	65,303
South Carolina	7,579	24,751	20,803	6,670	6,686	24,524
Georgia	12,025	36,962	53,112	14,800	15,184	55,550
Florida	16,920	41,960	42,548	13,715	13,364	52,799
Kentucky	9,671	34,573	819,216	49,911	37,497	101,325
Tennessee	9,076	33,156	316,357	50,915	30,245	110,675
Alabama	7,847	24,643	103,169	20,577	19,804	66,807
Mississippi	4,346	11,897	49,734	17,053	16,553	49,545
Arkansas	4,083	12,519	120,590	134,363	65,411	295,265
Louisiana	5,655	16,966	28,510	15,758	17,606	65,228
The South	113,974	382,132	1,728,603	358,492	256,684	953,844
Percent of White Population of the Division	1.1	1.2	5.2	2.4	3.9	4.9

SOURCE: United States Census of Population: 1960. Subject Reports, *State of Birth*, P.C.(2)-2A, Tables 18 and 19.

Table 8

White Population Five Years Old and Over Living in the South in 1955
By Selected Cities of Residence in 1960
City (SMSA) of Residence, 1960

PLACE OF RESIDENCE, 1955	CINCINNATI	CLEVELAND	COLUMBUS	DAYTON	INDIANAPOLIS	CHICAGO	DETROIT	LOS ANGELES	SAN FRANCISCO	NEW YORK
Virginia	1,936	2,894	2,022	2,332	1,105	6,638	3,439	10,444	5,478	7,762
North Carolina	941	1,278	761	583	622	3,825	2,079	8,005	2,079	4,855
South Carolina	386	407	360	334	213	1,590	802	2,152	1,196	2,177
Georgia	982	943	714	745	645	3,995	2,067	5,821	2,384	3,784
Florida	1,786	2,386	1,452	1,863	1,249	7,602	3,649	14,463	5,277	14,283
Kentucky	19,711	2,312	5,362	8,731	6,202	9,377	7,163	5,829	1,511	1,890
Tennessee	2,779	3,121	833	3,481	2,580	14,088	5,912	9,440	2,424	2,232
Alabama	441	809	566	749	470	6,907	1,978	4,765	1,830	1,661
Mississippi	245	201	324	257	296	4,948	531	2,816	1,170	848
Arkansas	159	270	189	119	552	5,267	1,094	10,077	2,958	628
Louisiana	290	366	532	385	304	2,058	710	5,877	2,518	1,881
The South	29,656	14,987	13,115	19,579	14,238	66,295	29,424	79,689	28,825	42,001

SOURCE: U.S. Census of Population: 1960. Subject Reports, *Mobility for Metropolitan Areas*, Final Report PC(2)-2C, Table 3.

Index

Abolitionism, 19–20, 39, 71–73
Adamic, Louis, 98, 118n
Akers, Elmer, 102, 107, 119n
Agriculture, 21, 27, 47, 50, 121
Agrarians, 29–30, 121
Americanism, and South, 120 23, 141
Anti-Catholicism, 76 77
Anti-Defamation League, 70, 81–82
Anti-Semitism, 74–77, 80–81
Appalachians, 13, 92–93, 101, 103, 106
Aristocracy, tradition of, 17, 45–50, 53
Arnall, Ellis, 7, 13n
Assimilation, 15, 123, 131; of Catholics, 78–79; of hillbillies, 112; of Jews, 78, 80
Association of Southern Women for the Prevention of Lynching, 35, 57

Beauregard, Pierre G. T., 72
Bender, Eugene I., 89n
Benjamin, Judah P., 73–74
Beynon, Erdmann D., 102, 119n
Black Power, 62, 65–66, 124–25 129–30
Black protest, 41, 88, 138
Blacks, 5, 7, 12, 14–17, 21–26, 29, 31, 34, 50, 53, 56–58, 63, 139; and Constitution, 129; employment, 59; in politics, 54, 57, 60–62, 64; as political minority, 127; in southern cities, 59
Blied, Benjamin J., 89n
Blumer, Herbert, 85, 90n
Bond, Julian, 60

Braden, William, 101, 119n
Brink, William, 146n
Broom, Leonard, 145n
Brown, Ina Corinne, 18, 42n
Brown, James S., 92–93, 118n
Brown, Malcolm J., 117n
Browne, Robert S., 130, 145n
Bruno, Hal, 117n
"Bumping days," 6

Cable, George Washington, 35
Caldwell, Erskine, 32
Calhoun, John C., 19, 126
Carmichael, Stokely, 126, 145n
Carpenter, Jesse T., 124, 129, 145n
Carpetbaggers, 5, 8, 23
Carter, Hodding III, 80, 90n
Cash, W. J., 8, 13n, 17, 42n, 46, 54–55
Catholics, 7, 12, 25, 37, 69, 70–71; and Confederacy, 71–72; and Ku Klux Klan, 76; and racial segregation, 88; and slavery, 70–71; in small towns, 78–79
Civil rights: Law of 1964, 57, 64, 86; movement, 6, 56, 58, 61, 64, 87, 131; workers, 6, 40, 64, 83–84
Civil War, 7, 9, 22, 47, 57; mythology of, 22
Class: lower, 13, 23, 25, 52–53; middle, 46, 48–50, 52; planter, 13, 16, 26, 45–48; upper, 52
Class structure, 26, 45–46, 49–53
Cleghorn, Reese, 146n
"Closed Society," 19, 39, 55
Collins, Henry Hill, 99, 118n

Colonized region, South as, 7, 27
Colony, hillbilly. *See* Ghettos
Commission on Interracial Cooperation, 57
Communism, 31, 40, 54
Concurrent majority, 126–28
Confederacy, 13, 20–21, 23, 71
Conservatives, white southern, 37, 54–55, 84
Constitution: Confederate, 71; Tenth Amendment, 125; U.S., 71–72, 121–22, 125, 127, 129
Cotton, 13–15, 19; mills, 48
Cultural traits, southern, 33

Dabbs, James M., 115, 118–19n, 133–34, 136, 146n
Deacons for Defense and Justice, 61
Dabney, Virginius, 28, 32, 43n
Danhof, Clarence H., 13n
Daniels, Jonathan, 7, 28, 43n
Davis, Jefferson, 20–22, 73
Defensive group consciousness, 4–5, 11–12, 20–21, 27, 33, 35, 37, 102, 144
Democratic Party, 37, 53–54, 62, 77, 121
Demagogues, 35, 53, 75
Depression, 25, 30, 36, 47, 50, 92
Desegregation. *See* Integration
"Dixie," 9–10, 22, 38, 65
Dixiecrat Party, 37, 78
Dunbar, Leslie, 134, 146n

Edmundson, Munro S., 85, 90n
Egerton, John, 133, 146n
Eisenhower, Dwight D., 77
"Eleanor Clubs," 6, 36
Ethnic groups, 16, 66, 69, 105, 107, 111, 143
Evers, Charles, 60

Faulkner, William, 32
Fichter, Joseph, 78, 90n
Forrest, Nathan B., 21–22
Frady, Marshall, 139, 146n
Frank, Leo, 75

Franklin, John Hope, 57, 68n
Foods, southern, 33, 116

Garrett, Henry, 143
Ghettos: black, 56, 58, 61, 86–87, 126, 128; hillbilly, 91, 102, 104–05, 112
Giffin, Roscoe, 119n
Ginzberg, Eli, 146n
Glazer, Nathan, 3, 13n
Glenn, Norval, 145n
Golden, Harry, 80
Goldwater, Barry, 140
Goodrich, Carter, 117n
Gordon, Milton, 122–23, 145n
Grady, Henry W., 27–28, 34
Graham, Frank P., 135–36, 146n
Grant, U. S., 22
Grantham, Dewey W., 4, 13n, 43n
Grigg, Charles, 68n
Grindstaff, Carl F., 68n

Hamilton, Charles V., 126, 128, 145n
Harris, Louis, 146n
Harris, Marvin, 10, 13n
Hauser, Philip, 59, 68n
Hawley, Amos, 102, 119n
Heberle, Rudolph, 46, 67n
Herrenvolk democracy, 122, 132
Hesseltine, William B., 27, 42–43n, 67n, 89n
Hillbillies, 11–12, 142n–43; in Chicago, 100–12; in Cincinnati, 102; in Detroit, 97–99, 102–03; discrimination against, 101, 108; in Flint, 102; in Indianapolis, 99; stereotypes of, 107–08, 111, 113
Hillbilly churches, 109–10
Hillbilly music, 106
Hillbilly taverns, 105–06, 109–11
Hillery, George A., Jr., 92–93, 118n
Horowitz, Irving, 138, 146n
Humphrey, Norman D., 99, 119n

Immigration, foreign, 15–16, 70, 72, 91
Indentured servants, 17–18
Industrialization, 16, 26–27, 29–31, 36–37, 47–49, 51, 121, 135; and blacks, 84–85, 135
Intelligence tests, 34, 143
Integration, racial, 29, 39, 41, 60, 64–65, 85, 130–32; of South into nation, 141
Interposition. *See* Nullification

Jackson, Andrew, 45, 120, 127, 137
Janson, Donald, 100, 105, 119n
Jefferson, Thomas, 120
Jews, 12, 15, 25, 69–70, 72; in Atlanta, 81–83; and Confederacy, 73–74; and Ku Klux Klan, 76; in New Orleans, 81; and segregation, 80–81, 88; and slavery, 73
Johnson, Gerald W., 114, 119n
Johnson, Lyndon B., 136
Johnson, Malcolm, 68n

Kaplan, Ben, 82, 90n
Karpinos, Bernard D., 146n
Kennedy, John F., 77, 136
Killian, Lewis, 68n, 119n
King, Martin Luther, Jr., 63, 131
Know-Nothing Party, 71
Kondracke, Morton, 101, 119n
Korn, Bertram W., 89n
Ku Klux Klan, 8, 23, 31, 38, 75–77

Labor unions, 30–31, 36, 85, 137
Lazarek, John R., 89n
Lee, Alfred M., 99, 119n
Lee, Howard, 60
Lee, Robert E., 21–22
Legends. *See* Myths
Lerche, Charles O., Jr., 53, 68n
Liebowitz, Martin, 138, 146n
Liberals, white southern, 7–8, 28, 33, 40, 70, 84, 114, 117, 122, 131, 134, 135–36
Linder, William H., 89n
Lippmann, Walter, 28

Liu, William T., 79, 83, 90n
Local self-government, 125
Lynching, 33, 75–76, 94; anti-lynching laws, 6, 35, 37

Matthews, Donald, 39–40, 44n
Mauldin, W. Parker, 117n
Maxwell, James, 99–100, 102, 119n
McCullers, Carson, 32
McGill, Ralph, 8, 13n, 28, 30, 31, 35, 43n, 90n, 136
McGurk, Francis, 143
Mechanization of agriculture, 50–51
Melting pot, 16, 123
Memorial Day, 22
Mencken, H. L., 94, 118n, 143
Metropolitan areas, 51, 53
Middleton, Russell W., 94–95, 118n
Migration: of blacks, 56–58, 62, 66; to farms, 50; selective, 92–93; from South, 11, 92–93; to South, 12, 83–84
Migrants: affluent, 113–16; working-class, 97, 100, 102–03
Miller, Herbert A., 40
Mind of the South, 54, 94
Minority: definition of, 4, 91; white southerners as, 37, 114
Minority rights, 123–24, 141
Minority protection, 131
Minority psychology. *see* Defensive group consciousness
Minorities, national, 11
Moore, Edmund A., 77, 89–90n
Moore, Wilbert E., 67n
Morland, J. Kenneth, 49, 67n
Morris, Willie, 96, 114, 116, 118–19n
Mountain whites, 13, 99–100, 103
Moynihan, Daniel P., 3, 13n
Myrdal, Gunnar, 67n
Myths: national, 141; Southern 21–23, 26, 134

Nam, Charles B., 92–93, 118n

National Association for the Advancement of Colored People, 40, 80, 129
Newfield, Jack, 129, 145n
New Left, 128, 135
Nicholls, William H., 48–49, 67n
Nixon, Richard M., 140
Norsworthy, David R., 85, 90n
Nouse, Dale, 98, 118n
Nullification, 38, 127, 129

Odum, Howard W., 7, 9, 13n, 16, 28, 32, 35–36, 42–43n, 92–93, 118n
One-party system, 53
Oppression psychosis, 40
"Outsiders," 36, 40, 64

Palmer, Vivien, 104, 119n
Participatory democracy, 128
Perkins, Frances, 32
Phillips, Ulrich B., 132
Plantation system, 18
Pluralism, 12, 123
Poll tax, 6, 37
"Poor whites," 13, 46, 49, 94, 106–07, 113, 143
Populist Party, 24, 34, 48
Powdermaker, Hortense, 46, 67n
Protestants, 3, 69, 71–72, 74–78, 88, 94, 142
Prothro, James, 39–40, 44n

Quasi-minority, 4, 142

Randel, William, 23, 42n
Randolph, A. Philip, 130
Ransom, John C., 43n
Reconstruction, 5, 8, 20–27, 36, 40, 47, 75
Reissman, Leonard, 49, 51, 67n
Regionalism, 9, 36
Religion, 3, 15, 18, 69–80, 88, 109–10, 121, 142
Republican Party, 37, 40, 53–54, 63, 77, 129, 136
Republic of New Africa, 56, 130
Resistance, southern, 37, 41, 53, 63

Roberts, Elizabeth Madox, 32
Roche, John P., 89n
Roosevelt, Franklin D., 7, 32, 50, 120
Rubin, Louis D., Jr., 43n
Rustin, Bayard, 130–31, 145n
Rural whites, 47, 49

Sanford, Gilbert A., 118n
Schermerhorn, R. A., 117n
Schrag, Peter, 137, 146n
Secession, 9, 13–15, 20, 23, 27, 70, 127, 130
Sectionalism, 8, 19, 30, 36–37
Segregation: of blacks, 5, 9–10, 18, 23–26, 34, 36–39, 41, 49, 53, 56–57, 60, 64, 116, 133; Catholics and, 78–79; de facto, 63–64, 132; Jews and, 80–81; of cotton mill workers, 49
"Separate but equal," 23, 37–38
Separatism, black, 130–31
Seligman, Ben B., 90n
Sherman, William T., 22
Shryock, Henry S., Jr., 92–93, 118n
Shuey, Audrey M., 143, 146n
Silver, James W., 39, 44n, 55
Simkins, Francis B., 145n
Slavery, 9, 13–19, 24–26, 46–47, 125, 129, 135
Smiley, David, 27, 42–43n, 67n, 89n
Smith, Alfred E., 37, 76
Smith, Lillian, 32, 69, 89n
South: definition of, 10–11; geography, 13, 15; population, 15–16, 50, 58; "New," 20, 27–28, 34, 54–55, 94; "Old," 20, 25–27, 33, 129, 135; "Solid," 6, 18, 20, 26, 76
Southern accent, 96–97, 107, 114–15
Southern gentlemen, 21, 48
Southern heritage, 11, 115, 134
"Southern mystique," 8, 26
"Southern Regional Council, 57, 60, 134
"Southern strategy," 140

Southern Student Organizing Committee, 135
Southern way of life, 23, 42
States' rights, 6–7, 19–20, 124
Stereotypes, 32, 144; of hill-billies, 102–23, 107–11; of Jews, 74; of "outsiders," 6; of South, 3, 32, 40, 103, 113–14
Students for a Democratic Society, 128, 135
Student Nonviolent Coordinating Committee, 128–29, 141
Supreme Court, U.S., 10, 37–39, 41, 56–57, 60, 62; *Dred Scott* decision, 71, 129, school desegregation decision, 57, 121, 125, 127
Sutker, Solomon, 82, 90n

Taney, Roger, 71
"Talent drag," 93–94, 96
Tariffs, 7, 19, 121, 127, 129
Tax abatements, 30, 84–85
Tenant farmers, 47, 50
Thomas, W. I., 144
Thompson, Daniel C., 34, 43n, 59, 68n
Thompson, Edgar, 35, 43n
Thompson, Warren S., 117n
Thurmond, J. Strom, 37, 62–63
Tobacco Road, 32
Tokenism, 41, 64
Topping, John C., Jr., 89n
Totalitarianism, 138–39
Tumin, Melvin, 39, 43n
Turner, Frederick Jackson, 9, 13n, 18, 42n

Universities, 6, 66, 84, 95–96
Urbanization, 26, 47–48, 50–51, 58–59; of blacks, 58–59; and

Catholics, 83; and Jews, 83; political effects of, 53

Vance, Rupert B., 42n
Van den Berghe, Pierre, 122, 142, 145–46n
Vander Zanden, James, 38, 43n
Violence, 39, 61, 138
Voting Rights Law of 1965, 60–62

Wagley, Charles, 10, 13n
Wallace, George C., 41, 46, 121, 136–37, 139–40
Washington, George, 17
"WASP," 3–4, 69, 81
Watson, Tom, 24–25, 75–76
Webb, John N., 177n
Wheeler, John H., 146n
White backlash, 87
White Citizens Council, 38, 80
White southerners: definition of, 11; marginal, 12, 70
White supremacy, 5, 20, 42, 54, 56, 134, 136, 142
Wilkins, Roy, 130
Williams, Robin M., 67n
Wirth, Louis, 4, 13n
Woodward, C. Vann, 20, 23, 26, 42–43n, 120, 134, 136, 145–46n
Woofter, T. J., Jr., 93
World War II, 35–36, 50

Yankees, 5–6, 22–23, 25–26, 29–32, 40, 48, 63, 69, 75; "transplanted," 83–88
Yoder, Edwin M., 54–55, 68n
Yulee, David, 73

Zinn, Howard, 141, 146n

About the Author

Lewis M. Killian is Professor of Sociology at the University of Massachusetts. He has also taught at the University of Connecticut, Storrs, The Florida State University, the University of Oklahoma, and the University of California at Los Angeles. Dr. Killian has contributed to many professional journals including the *American Sociological Review, Social Forces, Social Problems,* and *Phylon.* He is the co-author of *Collective Behavior* (1957) and *Racial Crisis in America* (1964). He is the author of *The Impossible Revolution?* (1968). He was born in Darien, Georgia, grew up in Macon, and attended the University of Georgia for his bachelor's and master's degrees.